A History of Music for Young People

RALPH VAUGHAN WILLIAMS ON THE ROSTRUM

The composer, at the age of eighty-two, conducting one of
his own works at the Royal Albert Hall.

By courtesy of the B.B.C.

A
History of Music
for Young People

by

JOHN RUSSELL
B.A. A.R.C.M. L.R.A.M.

SECOND EDITION
REVISED AND ENLARGED

GEORGE G. Harrap & CO. LTD
LONDON TORONTO WELLINGTON SYDNEY

First published in Great Britain 1957
by GEORGE G. HARRAP *&* CO. LTD
182 High Holborn, London, W.C.1

Reprinted: 1958; 1959; 1960; 1962

Second edition, revised and enlarged, 1965

This edition © *John Russell* 1965

*Composed in Linotype Caledonia type and printed by
Western Printing Services, Ltd, Bristol
Made in Great Britain*

Preface

THIS book is meant to be read as a story—the story of music's journey through the years. Dates have been kept out of it as much as possible; the lives of the composers have been merely touched upon; the names of several of them have not been mentioned, lest in a book of this nature the narrative resolve itself into a catalogue. It sets out to be a companion, rather than a textbook, for young people who are discovering music. It is hoped that through it they may catch a glimpse of the grandeur, the beauty, and the infinite variety of this great art they are beginning to explore.

My grateful thanks are due to Dr F. G. K. Westcott, H.M.I., for his valuable suggestions during the planning of this book; and to Alan Wykes for providing the index, and for his most generous professional guidance in the writing of the text.

J. R.

Preface to the Second Edition

NO book goes so quickly out of date as one which deals with a moving and changing art. Though I would devoutly wish to rewrite the whole of this book in the light of the increase of wisdom and judgment the years have brought me, I am none the less most grateful for the opportunity a new edition affords to correct, adjust, and expand.

First, an error of fact in Chapter 3 concerning the relationship between the Modes and Greek music has been corrected. This error (which could be seriously misleading to advanced students of the art) was due simply to my own ignorance at the time of writing, and I am indebted to Sir Ernest Bullock, lately Organist of Westminster Abbey and Director of the Royal College of Music, for pointing it out to me.

Secondly, it has been necessary to look again at the contemporary musical scene in England. In these days of immediate communication a mere eight years have seemed to establish two of our younger composers, Britten and Tippett, as important figures whose music reaches out far beyond these shores. For this reason it would appear necessary to say more about them than was relevant eight years ago.

Finally, I have been reminded that there are other ways of making music than the 'white-coloured' way. The peoples of India, the Far East, the West Indies, and Africa have made music since long before we discovered it, and for the same reasons. Much of their music can now be heard in films and in London recitals, and it is surely appropriate that we should leave room to consider how it is composed and played, for the entertainment of an increasing audience.

J. R.

May 1965

Contents

Illustrations

1

Musical History—How to Tackle it

O N THE following two pages there are two pieces of music. They are both to be sung by groups of voices, and they are both very often performed. There is not a great deal of difference in the way they are written down; they both show a similar arrangement of parallel lines and variously-shaped notes with words written under them, and if you were to hear them sung at this moment you might easily imagine that they were both written by the same composer.

There *is* a big difference between them, however: a difference of many centuries. The second tune was written during the Second World War; the one on the preceding page was written (less than a mile from where I am writing this) nearly seven hundred years ago. And within that seven hundred years lies nearly all the music of the entire Western World that any ordinary reader need bother about. Compared with the history of even one particular country, the history of music is a short, orderly one.

In the history of a country it is, of course, quite important to know in what year a king came to the throne, when an Act of Parliament was passed, and when battles were fought. Only in this way can we get a clear idea of the happenings which in some way or other have altered the course of people's lives. For most students the nastiest part of history is the incessant learning and memorizing of dates. What a bore it can be, especially when they are all the dates of "far-off things, and battles long ago."

In the history of music dates become quite manageable. For instance, there is really not much point in learning in

Sumer is icumen in (medieval)

what year a composer was born. He wouldn't be writing music for quite a time—though Mozart was composing little pieces when he was not quite five. What is important, however, is to know in what *period* the composer was writing his music: that is to say, whether it was in the sixteen-hundreds, for instance, or the middle seventeen-hundreds, or the late eighteen-hundreds. If you can learn as much as that, you can link up the *sound* of one composer's music with that of another. You can say, "This music is like that music," meaning that both pieces were written by composers who used the same musical

Round the Earth a Message runs (twentieth century)

language, because it was the language of the time in which they lived; or you can say, "This music is different from that music," and you will know that the difference is due to the fact that one piece of music was written at an earlier or a later time than the other. You can also find links between the sound of music and other 'ways of expression' of the time in which it was written—the way people dressed, built houses, made furniture, painted pictures.

Though it is quite *interesting* to learn, for instance, that two very great composers, Bach and Handel, were both born in 1685, it is much more *important* to know that their music was the finest that was being produced during the first fifty years of the seventeen-hundreds, and to know why it was so. Again, though the popular and beloved composers Chopin, Schumann, and Mendelssohn were all born round about 1810, and were all dead and gone by 1856, those dates simply do not matter provided you realize that the music of these composers was the mainstay of the musical world throughout the entire span of the last hundred years, and, together with music by composers of slightly later date, is still the easiest and most enjoyable music to listen to in the early stages of your listening. If you think of musical history in 'slabs' like this you will find that in a surprisingly short time you can hear a piece of music and say at once, "That must be Bach," or, "That is music of Mozart's time," or "Surely that is Romantic music" (meaning that it must have been written in the earlier part of the eighteen-hundreds). In other words you are using your knowledge of musical history to enable you to 'place' the music you hear in its surroundings, and even to make an intelligent guess at the name of the composer.

At this point look again at the music at the beginning of this chapter. The first piece of music, *Sumer is icumen in*, is an extraordinarily fine choral song. The tune is a delight to sing, the voices are woven together in a most ingenious way, and the mood is gloriously joyous and spring-like. It is, moreover, so much more musical and more skilfully written down than any other music we know from those far-off times that we are quite liable to tell ourselves that it is a freak. We imagine that the composer (thought to be one John of Fornsete, a clerk at Reading Abbey) suddenly composed *Sumer is icumen in* in a burst of joy one fine spring morning, and that he and his music were something that 'just happened.' But from whom did he learn how to write down the music he heard in his head? What has happened to the music of other people which must have sounded around him?

CHAMBER MUSIC, "THE MUSIC OF FRIENDS"
A string quartet rehearses. In front are the two violins,
behind them the cello and viola.
By courtesy of the B.B.C.

THE OPERA ORCHESTRA REHEARSES
By courtesy of the B.B.C.

SOME WOODWIND INSTRUMENTS

Two flutes and an oboe are in front, two clarinets behind them,
and a bassoon is on the right. A cor anglais stands within reach
of the oboist.

By courtesy of the B.B.C.

SOME BRASS AND PERCUSSION INSTRUMENTS

Two French horns are in front, two trumpets behind them, and
three trombones at the back. A timpanist is on the right.

By courtesy of the B.B.C.

Why was John of Fornsete's song so popular in those days (we know it must have been, because it has devotional Latin words as well as jolly English ones)? What probably did happen was that the 'Reading Rota,' as this song is sometimes called, came down to us partly by accident, and partly because it was some of the very best music to be written at that time. As we follow the course of music up to the present day we find again and again that the finest music of each period has been the work of only a few composers, sometimes only two or three of them. The music of these few has 'come to stay' because it was the best of its time, and that of scores of other composers living at the same period has been washed away on the tide of time, leaving merely a mention of their names in musical dictionaries and perhaps a heap of lifeless music-paper which has never had its contents played or sung since the time when it was written.

On the other hand, there are some musicians along the line of history whose music does not perhaps take them to the highest places of importance, but who have in some way or other pointed the way ahead for greater men. The jet airliner, cruising majestically through the upper atmosphere thousands of feet above the Atlantic Ocean, is a most wonderful and impressive achievement, but as an *idea* it is far from new. If such men as the Wright brothers and Blériot had not made their ramshackle machines leave the ground the jet airliner would not have left the ground either. Yet though many of you could give a very accurate description of the size, shape, and mechanism of a modern airliner, there must be few of you who could be as accurate about the aeroplane which brought Colonel Lindberg across the ocean and set him down in Europe, a godlike visitor from another planet.

As we watch music growing, we find we must guard against forgetting about the pioneers, just because they may not have written music we know and like. So in this book they will be taken care of by being given a chapter to themselves from time to time, which I will call a

'Signpost.' These musicians provided music with important *ideas*, though some of them might not have been sufficiently talented, profound, or appealing as composers for their music to take its place in the main thoroughfare. The great ones, nevertheless, often became great because they were able by their genius to develop and expand the new ideas into the 'jet airliner' music that lives and flourishes for our delight.

Do not skip the 'Signpost' chapters, because you cannot form a really useful impression of the musical scene if you do. You might discover, for instance, that the sound of music and the ways of writing it change very suddenly in a very short time. In fact there is as great a difference between the last music J. S. Bach wrote and the first that Mozart wrote barely ten years later as there is between the English language and the German language. Why is this? How did it happen? The 'Signpost' chapters will help you to understand these things. They will also act as 'bridges' between one slab of time (and its music) and the next one.

2

Ways of making Music

ALL people who have specialized jobs, whether they be farmers, electricians, or fishermen, have their own tools of the trade, and their own ways of describing their work. This chapter will tell you, very briefly, the main ways in which a musician makes his music, and how he talks about it.

When you come to think about it, there are only two ways of making music: singing and playing. We either make sounds with our voices, or we produce them from instruments which we strike, stroke, or blow.

Our voices are, of course, the earliest musical instruments we know anything about. We soon learn that by making our voices go up and down we can produce a *tune*; if we 'put some words in' the tune becomes a *song*. If we sing while we are walking or dancing our song will most likely keep time with our movements; we will *step on* some words or notes a little more strongly than on others, so that our song, besides having a tune, has another aspect of music added to it, called *rhythm*.

One voice, then, can make music which has tune, words, and rhythm. Two voices, each singing different tunes at the same time, can take music a step farther. If the two tunes are built for each other so that they will fit together like the cogwheels in a gearbox they are said to *harmonize*, giving us *harmony*.

There are two main kinds of voice: a man's voice and a woman's voice. If these two voices sing in harmony the music again becomes richer and more interesting; it has been given variety of tone-quality, which is usually spoken of as *tone-colour*.

Some men find that their voices sound better on high notes, and others prefer low notes. The high voice has a tone-colour of its own and is called *tenor*, and so has the low voice, which is called *bass* (pronounced 'base').

There is the same difference in women's voices. Here the high voice is called *soprano*, and the low voice *contralto*.

If a soprano, a contralto, a tenor, and a bass all sing different tunes in harmony the music is the richer for having four different tone-colours in it. These are the four main types of voice used to make music. To complete the list we can add one or two more.

A boy's voice, before it changes into a man's, can sing soprano music; but it is usually called treble, to show that it is, in fact, a male voice.

Some men find that they can produce their best tone half-way between the tenor and bass sounds; their voice is called *baritone*. Some women, too, have voices half-way between soprano and contralto; this voice is called *mezzo-soprano*.

The Range of the Various Types of Voice

Finally we must include a voice not often heard nowadays, but one of very great importance to anyone who follows the fortunes of singers throughout musical history. This is the *alto*, which is the male version of the contralto. With careful training and practice, a man with a normal tenor or baritone voice can give the notes he sings a contralto tone-colour and range of notes—which is very useful in church choirs and other religious gatherings where no place can be found for female voices. We shall see later on that this type of male voice was the mainstay of the great cathedral choral music, and of the opera too, a few hundred years ago; so important was it that a great many boys were made to undergo a surgical operation which ensured that, as they grew to manhood their voices remained unchanged.

Women { SOPRANO   Mezzo-Soprano
CONTRALTO

Men { TENOR   Treble (before change of voice)
          Baritone   Alto
BASS

If there are lots of sopranos, contraltos, tenors and basses all singing together in harmony they make a *chorus* or *choir*.

A singer, therefore, can make music in several ways:

1. He can sing by himself, or with some one accompanying him on the piano (*solo*).

2. He can join in with another singer (*duet*), or with two others (*trio*), or with three others (*quartet*), and so on.

3. He can sing with a crowd of other singers (*chorus* or *choir*).

4. He can put on fancy dress and grease-paint, go on the stage, and sing and act at the same time, together with many other people doing the same thing (*opera*).

5. He can sit round the table with a few friends and sing madrigals. More about that later.

Music is a friendly art; it depends a great deal (just as friends do) on harmony, that 'getting-together' of makers of music to produce harmonious sound. As we all have only one voice, however, we can only make one tune at a time; but we do have ten fingers. It was not long, therefore, before musicians discovered how to make a musical

instrument from which one person with his ten fingers—
and sometimes his two feet—could draw music which
had both tune *and* harmony.

Such an instrument was worked by a *keyboard*, a row
of keys each of which caused a note to sound when the
player pressed it. In pressing—or striking—the key, a
delicate piece of machinery was set in motion which
caused a wire to vibrate, or which allowed some air to
blow down a pipe. There, in their beginnings, were the
piano in your home and the organ in church.

But the piano is a youngster, compared to the organ; it
is less than 250 years old. In fact, when it was first invented, a famous musician of the time sneered at it as
being "only fit for light music." There had been several
excellent "piano-type" instruments long before, which
had inspired all the finest composers to write some of
their best music for them; but they did not work in quite
the same way. Here are the two most important ones—
as you will see, their mechanisms differ from that of the
piano:

The Clavichord. In this instrument when a key is struck
a piece of metal, called a tangent, is pushed up against
the string, causing it to vibrate and make a sound. The
sound is a very tiny one, and makes you listen very in-
tently, but it is so beautiful that it is well worth the effort.
Now, if you look inside a piano while you strike a key
you will see that a hammer strikes the string, and immediately *bounces off again,* so that once you hear the note
there's nothing whatever you can do to alter it. On the
clavichord, however, the tangent does not bounce off; it
stays pressed up against the string, so that if, for instance,
you wobble your finger on the key when you strike it the
sound wobbles too. So that on the clavichord you get a
tiny sound which you can control while it lasts; but on
the piano you get a much, much bigger sound which you
can do nothing about once you've heard it.

The Harpsichord. This is by far the most famous of the
pre-piano 'hammer-and-strings' instruments, but its

mechanism is very different from that of the piano. When a key is struck a sharp piece of quill darts up to the string, *plucks* it, and then falls back into place again. So, once again, there's nothing to be done about the sound once you've hit the key. More important, though, is the fact that you can do very little to make loud or soft sounds (by causing a vigorous 'pluck' or a gentle one) whereas on the piano you can at least make the hammer hit the string hard or gently.

Though the actual fingers of the player cannot make much difference to the sound of a harpsichord, differences can be achieved in the following ways:

1. The harpsichord has two keyboards; you may play either one separately, or play one with the other 'coupled,' or linked, to it, so that both sound simultaneously, producing a rich effect. You need them too to play some of the music written for the harpsichord, if you don't want to get your fingers hopelessly tangled up. In some makes of harpsichord it is possible to achieve a difference in volume and tone-quality between the two keyboards.

2. There are various stops and pedals which cause two or more notes to sound when you strike only one key, and which vary the number of strings which are struck for each note; this in turn varies the volume of sound.

3. The plucking is done sometimes with quills and sometimes with tiny strips of leather (both on the same piece of wood, and changed by pressing a pedal).

Other keyboard instruments which worked in much the same way, but which were smaller and simpler, were the *virginals* (out of date by about 1650) and the *spinet* (which was still to be found in use over a hundred years after that date).

So we can think of the harpsichord, the virginals, and the spinet as cousins of the piano. The clavichord, however, was so similar in the way it worked that it appears these days to be a sort of wizened old grandfather of the piano—one of the same family.

The Organ. If people who do not like the organ wish to sneer at it they often call it a "box of whistles"—which is exactly what it is! When you press a key, a gust of wind is blown into a pipe, which gives out a sound. This keyboard instrument is by far the oldest of them all. It was used for sacred occasions long before the birth of Christ, and it was in fact quite a complicated musical instrument three hundred years before anyone thought of the harpsichord.

It is the most highly 'mechanized' instrument of all. As the years have gone on it has had added to it countless devices to give it richer and more varied tone-colour. Several keyboards (up to five or six), a pedal keyboard (to be played with the feet), hundreds of stops (which bring various pipes into play, all having different tone-colours), couplers (linking up the keyboards), pistons (combining groups of stops so that they can all be operated from one keyboard), 'swell-boxes' (enclosing groups of pipes, and having shutters which can be opened gradually to let the sound out bit by bit, thus producing, by mechanized means, crescendo and diminuendo effects): these are by no means all of the mechanical gadgets of the organ. And yet, with all these mechanical aids, the player who presses the keys has no control whatever over the quality, or the loudness and softness, of the tone. He can lean his elbow on the key, or touch it with the tip of his finger, and the sound will be precisely the same. The important thing is, however, that the note will go on sounding just as it did at its beginning for as long as the player keeps his finger on the key; and that is the main difference between the organ and all the other keyboard instruments. That is what gives the organ the solid, sustained tone which can fill an enormous cathedral and lead great crowds of people to sing together. The good organist has to use all his skill to produce variety of tone (through his artistic use of combinations of stops) and clarity of sound (through being able to judge just when he should *release* the key in order to finish the notes he is playing).

There, then, are the main points about keyboard instruments, upon which we can make music which is complete in itself, having rhythm, tune, harmony, and tone-colour.

When we strike a note on the piano we cause a string to vibrate by hitting it with a hammer. We can also cause a string to vibrate by drawing over it a bunch of horsehair, stretched out along the length of a piece of wood, which is called a bow. This is how we play the *violin*, the *viola*, the *violoncello* (*cello*), and the *double bass*, and this group of instruments is called the *strings*.

The *violin* is the smallest stringed instrument. It has four strings which give these notes:

Any other notes have to be made by the player, who shortens the strings by pressing his fingers on them at various places.

The *viola* is a little larger but, like the violin, it can be held under the player's chin. It also has four strings, which give these notes:

The viola has a peculiar sound—a dark, chilly one, but oddly haunting and attractive, like a winter landscape. It is also quite the most useful of all the stringed instruments. Every orchestra must have several of them, and viola-players are always in demand.

The *violoncello* (usually called by its abbreviation, *cello*) is the father of the string family. It is large and bulky, and must stand on the floor in a dignified manner. Its four strings give these notes:

The *double-bass* must surely be the grandfather. It also stands on the floor, of course, and the player has to stand too, to reach all the notes he wants to play. It has four strings nowadays, giving:

each of these notes sounding an octave lower than it is written; but it took a long time to settle down to this. Quite a lot of the older instruments had only three strings, and these were 'tuned' to all sorts of patterns of notes. You will notice that the double-bass strings are tuned at intervals of four notes (*i.e.*, in 'fourths'), whereas those of the rest of the String Family are tuned at intervals of five notes (*i.e.*, 'fifths'). All these stringed instruments work in the same way. A composer can ask the player to produce various different sounds from them by putting instructions in Italian on the music, as follows:

Arco. Play by drawing the bow over the strings.

Pizzicato. Pluck the strings with the finger.

Con sordino. Clip a little metal gadget on to the 'bridge' (the curved piece of wood which holds the strings up). This cuts down the vibrations, and gives a thin, veiled sound, quite different from the one we usually hear. The gadget is called a 'mute,' and we talk about 'muted strings.'

Sul ponticello. Play with the bow very near the bridge. This produces a steely, rough tone which is needed occasionally.

Col legno. Turn the bow over and play with the wooden part. This causes a sharp rattle on each note.

Although a string-player can 'play a duet with himself' by playing on two strings at the same time, he is usually just playing one line of music. Just like a singer, he has to get together with other players if he wants to play 'in harmony,' but what a wonderful time he can have! He can play in an orchestra, getting to know a vast and varied amount of music, or he can meet with a few of his kind and play string quartets after tea; and all the while the poor pianist is plodding along alone. No orchestra wants him, because there is no part for him to play, and string-players would much rather do without him in their quartet-playing, as he is inclined to make too much noise.

The organist makes his music by causing air to be blown through a pipe. While he achieves this by pressing a key, others blow with their own mouths through their piped instruments. These instruments are made of either wood or metal; the wood ones are called *woodwind*, and the metal ones *brass*. The commonest woodwind instruments are the *flute*, the *oboe*, the *clarinet*, and the *bassoon*.

The *flute* is the highest and most delicate of them all. It is played held crosswise, while all the others are blown downward.

The *oboe* owes its piercing, nasal tone to the fact that the player blows between two narrow strips of cane (like two leaves of grass) called 'reeds.'

The *clarinet* has a smooth, oily tone, and has just one reed, wider and larger than the oboe's.

The *bassoon* has a warm, comical, affectionate sound, like an old man's voice. It is too long to allow the player to blow down it from the top, so it has a curved metal tube sticking out sideways, about a third of the way down. This is fitted with a double reed, like the oboe.

That is the woodwind family, arranged like the soprano, alto, tenor, and bass of the choir.

The brass instruments consist of the *french horn*, the *trumpet*, the *trombone*, and the *tuba*.

The *french horn*, though a very difficult instrument to play, produces some of the most beautiful sounds in music. It can be melting and romantic when it plays a tune, or stirring and martial when several of them play sharply and loudly. It is about eleven feet long, but it is coiled up so that the player can hold it under his elbow and blow into it comfortably.

The *trumpet*, with its 'bright red' sound, has not got the variety of tone of the french horn, but it can always be relied on to give colour and brilliance to music.

The *trombone* produces its noble notes by being shortened or lengthened. The player pushes and pulls a sliding tube, and is able to 'feel' where the notes are.

The *tuba* is the somewhat grumpy grandfather of the brass family. It is a bulky instrument which sits on the player's knee, and is *not* to be confused with the one which curls like a boa-constrictor round his neck, ending with a huge polished horn. That is an American instrument which does not concern us, though it is sometimes thought of as a tuba.

Finally there are the drums, or rather the *percussion* or 'hitting' instruments. There are a great many of these, used by composers to make special effects, but we need only think about three of them; the *timpani*, the *side drum*, and the *bass drum*.

The *timpani* are large copper basins which look like cauldrons. They have a layer of skin stretched across the top which can be tightened or loosened by screwing or unscrewing taps around the edges. This skin is hit by sticks with soft, felt ends. As you see, you can *tune* these drums to various notes. That is what the drummer is doing when he can be seen leaning over the drum, tapping it, and frantically turning the taps in the middle of the music. The timpani (or 'timps,' as they are often called for short) are sometimes known as *kettle-drums*.

The *side drum* is the smallest of the drum family, round and cylindrical with a layer of parchment stretched over each end. Across one end are stretched several strands of wire or catgut, called 'snares,' which vibrate against the parchment when it is hit with wooden sticks; the other end is left clear. The dry, military rattle of the side drum is an exciting sound in orchestral music.

The *bass drum* is a large version of the side drum, without the snares, and stands on its side. When it is hit with a soft-ended stick it gives off a thrilling, booming note, a sort of 'bottomless pit' of sound.

As well as these drums the percussion department (or the 'kitchen,' as orchestral players affectionately call it) contains numbers of things such as the *tambourine*, *cymbals*, *triangle*, *gong*, *castanets*, *bells*, and *rattles*, all of which can contribute to the excitement of the music.

Now that we know something about the main musical instruments it is time to see how they were put together to make the greatest instrument of all: the *orchestra*. When you go to a full orchestral concert these days the orchestra will always look the same, whichever orchestra it may be. There will be the usual array of strings along the front of the platform, the percussion, with its gleaming timpani, will be somewhere at the back, and so will the legions of brass, with the trombones giving themselves plenty of room for the manipulating of their slides. In between will be the woodwind, usually in tidy groups of two per instrument. The pattern you see before you is the one that the composer sees in his mind when he writes a piece of orchestral music, and he is thinking of the sounds of the instruments we have been reading about. He will sit down at his pages of music-paper, and will write out his music so that the following instruments have parts to play: two flutes, two oboes, two clarinets, two bassoons; four french horns, two trumpets, three trombones, one tuba; percussion; twelve first violins, ten second violins, eight violas, eight 'cellos, six double-basses (the numbers of strings vary, but this is a normal layout). It doesn't matter how many strings there are—the more the better—and they are also grouped in twos, though each sort of instrument plays the same line of music.

The composer writes out the parts for all these instruments in a *score*, one part below the other. A page of music from a score, therefore, can show all the orchestra playing at once.

But let us suddenly think back 350 years, and try and imagine the sort of orchestra we would find. We are in Mantua, in Italy, about to hear a performance of an opera by a great composer, Monteverde. The orchestra at first looks rather like a furniture shop. There are three harpsichords, three little organs (like harmoniums), a harp, a mixture of flutes, trumpets, trombones, oboes, and a cluster of stringed instruments. In fact, anyone in the neighbourhood who could play any instrument at all had been told to bring it along. The composer then wrote some music to fit them.

Now let us drop in to a concert about 120 years later. Here is Bach, rehearsing his orchestra for a performance in St Thomas's Church in Leipzig. He is sitting at the harpsichord, and around him are the string family— violins, violas, cellos, and double-basses. These are obviously the backbone of the orchestra, but beside them are several woodwind instruments (but no clarinets as yet), in groups of two, and trumpets and drums. The picture looks a little more familiar, but the harpsichord seems to be the centre of activity. From his seat at the keyboard Bach is not only directing the players, he himself is playing most of the time, *accompanying* the rest of them. The harpsichord is going *continuously*, holding all the others together, and its part in the proceedings is actually called the *continuo*. Bach and his fellow-composers only wrote down the bare bass part of the music (*i.e.*, the part played by the cellos and double-basses) for the continuo player, who had to make up the rest of his part as he went along. The player was helped by numbers written above or beneath his part which showed him what the harmony should be. His job was to support the other players and singers. When the orchestra begins to play we soon notice that there is not much difference between the tunes the strings play and those the wood-wind and brass play. They are all 'doubling' each other.

Our next port of call is a concert in Vienna in 1800. Beethoven is conducting his First Symphony. The harpsi-chord, and indeed any keyboard instrument, has gone for ever. There is no longer any need to 'fill in' the middle of the music with a continuo part: that is being done by the woodwind and the brass in orderly groups, two each of flutes, oboes, clarinets, bassoons, horns, and trumpets. It is so much more interesting a filling-in too, as all these instruments bring their different sounds and colours to the music. During the hundred years between Bach and Beethoven a lot of experimenting had been done by composers. They were ceaselessly looking for variety and colour, and they all gradually settled on the orchestral pattern of strings, and the wind forces we have just mentioned. For that sort of orchestra was written all the orchestral music of Haydn and Mozart, and most of Beethoven's. (The timpani were used regularly by Beethoven and his successors, but not in by any means all the works by Haydn and Mozart.)

At this point, however, orchestral composers began to show signs of going quite mad. It all started harmlessly enough. Composers found that they wanted more and deeper noise from the orchestra, so they began regularly to use trombones, and later the tuba as well. To balance these additions, they found they had to have four horns instead of two, and then they had to use more of the string family. A concert of 1900, therefore, would find us looking at a large, swollen orchestra, with a much larger brass section, giving forth music by Tchaikovsky which was extremely rich, colourful, and noisy, but still balanced in sound. There wasn't too much of any instrument, and the orchestra was still able to get on to the platform, even with a bit of a squeeze. But why not have a bigger orchestra still? Why not have four of all the woodwind, eight each of the brass, a hundred of the strings? On it went, until by about 1910 an orchestra looked like a battalion going into action, and our ears became stunned and deadened under the blows of the blaring brass and the battering drums. There were all sorts of extra instruments too, some of which will be listed at the end of this chapter. This inflation could not go on; it was not leading anywhere except to bigger orchestras still, which nobody could afford to pay. Nowadays composers have again come to their senses, and find that they can write the music they want perfectly well for nothing bigger than the Tchaikovsky orchestra. One of the first composers to see reason in this respect was Sibelius, the great Finnish composer, who has given us music with great power in it which he gets from the normal nineteenth-century orchestra.

The modern symphony orchestra has come about, therefore, through three hundred years of experiment. It has settled down as an instrument on which to make music, just as a piano has music drawn out of it by the pianist. If a composer wishes to write a piece of orchestral music he has just as clear a sound of an orchestra in his mind as a piano composer has of the sound of the piano.

The orchestra, then, is a musical instrument. Who plays it? It used to be the man at the keyboard—the harpsichord continuo-player; now, of course, it is the *conductor*

The conductor, looking down at his score, can see what every one ought to be playing. He is the only man who can see this, as all the players have just their own part in front of them. It is his job to turn his score, a complex 'blueprint' of instruments, voices, and the composer's instructions, into musical sound—the sound the composer heard in his head when he wrote it all down. He must see that all his eighty or ninety players play as one— that they keep together as closely as the two hands of a pianist. He must indicate the speed, the loudness and softness, and the *mood* of the music, and he can do this in only one way, by the movement of his hands, arms, and head. He must rely completely on *gesture*.

The conductor has 'gone up' in the world of music. He is worshipped just as much by audiences as great singers and pianists were in the past. But only 150 years ago he was inclined to be thought of as a necessary evil, merely engaged in keeping every one together. To do this he would beat with a stick on the stand in front of him, or even thump on the floor with a sort of broomstick. Lully, a great French composer, was doing this one day when he thumped his toe instead, and died of blood-poisoning. Nowadays the conductor is a godlike creature, whose elegant, fiery, graceful gestures are all directed towards hypnotizing the orchestra—and the audience—while the music is going on.

Finally, to complete our picture of the modern symphony orchestra, here are a few extra instruments, visitors to the main family, which are nevertheless often to be found at concerts:

The *piccolo*, a very small flute, bright and shrill. Played by the man who plays the second flute.

The *cor anglais*, an elder member of the oboe family. It has a haunting, dark tone (like the viola, it has a melancholy sound) and is used for expressive solos. Listen sometime to Dvořák's 'New World' Symphony, or Sibelius's *The Swan of Tuonela*, both of which have typical cor anglais solos in them. It is usually played by the second oboist.

The *bass clarinet*, sounding an octave lower than the clarinet, has a hollow, oily, rather sinister sound in its lower notes. It has been nicknamed the 'bass goblin.'

The *double-bassoon* is a fine sight on the platform—it looks like a rather complicated drainpipe. Its lowest notes (which are lower than those of any other instrument in the orchestra) have a coarse, 'edgy,' but firm tone.

The *harp* is always a welcome visitor. Its part comes just below that of the percussion in the score.

The *piano* is *very* rarely found in an orchestra, unless it has a big solo part to play, accompanied by the orchestra—*i.e.*, in a *concerto*. In that case, its part is found just above that of the strings in the score.

The *chorus* (if there are singing parts in the music) is also found just above the strings in the score.

3

The Early Days

NEARLY all the music you sing and play and listen to has been written during the last two hundred years. The School Choir might sing one or two songs by composers who were writing before 1700, such as Purcell's "Fairest Isle" and "Sound the Trumpet"; the Recorder Group and the Madrigal Society will most certainly dip into the music of Byrd, Morley, and Gibbons, belonging to the 1500–1600 period; and one or two of your morning assembly hymns, such as "Sing, my tongue, the glorious battle," or "O come, O come, Emmanuel," take you back for the moment farther than that. Even so you are considerably luckier than the average adult listener, whose chances of hearing in the concert-hall any music before Bach and Handel are very slim indeed.

Why is this? The main reason is that, as the centuries go by, we *listen* differently. People gradually get tired of the older music as it recedes farther and farther into the past. It no longer makes them feel happy or sad; it ceases to move them. They get out of touch with its moods, because composers have come along since who have spoken more clearly and sympathetically through their music. They have used richer sounds, bigger orchestras, longer tunes, louder noises, and in doing so they *mean* more to us.

Sometimes, however, just as we find that we have ruled out some old music because we think it is out of date, we get a surprise. When Bach died in 1750 already people were calling his music out of date. They much preferred the new type of music (the Mozart kind) that was coming over from Italy. It was nearly a hundred years later that another German composer, Mendelssohn, brought Bach's music back to life by performing it at concerts. Since then, not only have nearly *all* musicians regarded him as the greatest composer who has ever lived, but thousands of ordinary listeners flock to hear his music because they find such great joy and satisfaction in it—and, after all, it is for that that anyone listens to music.

We know that for at least three thousand years people have used music as we use it now—to express feelings that cannot be fully expressed in words. With it they have welcomed victorious armies, soothed children to sleep, consoled themselves when they were sad; they danced to it, worshipped their gods with it, and to sad laments they buried their dead. We know about this because of pictures and drawings which have been discovered among the ruins of older civilizations, showing the musicians and their instruments. These instruments, all either plucked, blown, or banged, are often quite beautifully and elaborately made, which means that people must have been making them for a long time previously. Most of these pictures were found in Egypt and in the Mediterranean countries, and with them we can trace the rapid growth of music right up to about a thousand years before Christ, the time when the Jewish temples were resounding with singing and large orchestras. How do we know this? Turn to your Bibles and read the Psalms, especially Nos. 81 and 150, and make a list of the instruments used to the glory of God: harp, trumpet, cymbals, timbrel (a small tambourine), psaltery (dulcimer), stringed instruments, organ, choruses ("Let everything that hath breath praise the Lord."). It must have been a grand sound—a "joyful noise."

At the same time music was being taken very seriously in Greece. Not only was it being used to celebrate important events, or to soothe people, but it was held to have the same uses as medicine or tonics; the mentally sick were comforted and healed by it, and those already in good health found it helped them to lead richer and fuller lives. At first most of this music consisted of songs; singers told long stories of bravery, and wove legends round their gods, by singing them to the accompaniment of a harp. Later, music played on instruments was used as background to their plays, just as we use 'incidental music' in the theatres nowadays. The most important thing the Greeks did for music, however, was to work out a system for writing it down, so that it could be played again and again.

The only trace left by the Greeks on our music is a series of Greek names borrowed by early church musicians to describe the scales, or sequences of notes, on which they built their tunes and chants. There were seven of these sequences, as compared with the two scales upon which most of the music we know is built; *God save the Queen* is built on one, the major, and *The Miller of Dee* is built on the other, the minor. But the early church musicians had seven different scales. You can play them for yourselves on the piano by starting on any white key and playing to the octave above, using nothing but the white keys all the way. Only once will you make a sound like the "doh, ray, me, fah, soh, lah, te, doh" that you know so well. All the others will sound a little strange. These scales were called "modes," and they were given such pleasant-sounding Greek names as *Lydian, Æolian, Ionian, Dorian.* But these you need not bother about, except the last one, which we will examine just so that you have some idea how these modes worked. Sing up the scale, but start not on "doh" but on "ray"—"ray, me, fah, soh, lah, te, doh, ray"—or put your finger on D on the piano and play all the white notes until you get to the D an octave higher. There you have a mode: the *Dorian* mode. Now sing to yourself that rollicking sea shanty, "What shall we do with a drunken sailor?" You will notice that all the notes you sing in that song are included in the Greek scale you have just played or sung—the Dorian mode. Perhaps you have noticed before that that particular tune does seem to skate up and down in rather an unusual way. There's something rather old-fashioned and *antique* about music written in a mode.

"What shall we do with a drunken Sailor?"

Only now do we come to the beginning of our calendar —the birth of Christ, very nearly two thousand years ago. As He proceeded to set up His Church it became obvious that music was going to play a part in it, and behind Him there was this vast knowledge of Jewish and Greek music to put into use. ("And when they had *sung an hymn*, they went out into the mount of Olives.")

For the first thousand years of our calendar the art of music grew up with the rise of the Christian Church; their stories are the same. Church music began with the chanting of prayers and hymns to tunes in the Greek style, and was known as *plainsong*. Plainsong is still used very widely in churches, especially Catholic ones, and it is fascinating to sing. It is so much freer and more flexible than the usual hymn-tunes. If you use *The English Hymnal* at school or in church try singing No. 1, "Creator of the stars of night," or No. 264 (the second tune), "Before the ending of the day." Just sing to the end of each line before you take a breath; don't accent any word or note, let the music slow down and die away at the end of each verse, and let the words wander along as if you were just saying them. If you can manage all that you will sound just like a monk in some monastery chapel fifteen hundred years ago—or only yesterday!

So far there had been one striking difference between the music of those days and that which we know now. Every one, when they made music together, played or sang the same tune. All music was in *unison*. It was not until about A.D. 800 that church musicians found out that if all the men in the choir sang one tune and all the boys another, *at the same time*, they could produce richer and more interesting music. From then onward singing in parts (*polyphony*) became more and more elaborate, starting with only two parts singing at a distance of four (or five) notes apart (*i.e.*, in a succession of 'fourths' or 'fifths') and progressing until, in about 1550, a composer called Thomas Tallis managed to write music with no fewer than forty parts going all at once.

Although this discovery of part-singing made music richer than it had ever been before, it did not mean that singers did not sing solo or unison songs any more. At the same time as church musicians were exploring polyphony there was growing up, in France and Germany, a great love of melodious, poetic song among the knights and the nobility. These aristocrats had not only to be able to ride horses, joust with lances, and rescue damsels in distress, they must also be able to compose tender little songs, both words and music, and sing them themselves, accompanying themselves on the lute or the harp. These musicians were called *troubadours* or *trouvères* (according to whether they lived in the south or in the centre and north) in France, and *Minnesingers* in Germany. To make music like this was an important thing for the nobility to do, just as playing a good game of golf or riding with the local hunt would be to-day. If they were not very good at singing and playing, or did not like performing in public, they employed professional musicians, called minstrels, to sing their songs for them. The Minnesingers, in particular, were very fond of competing against each other in song, just as we do now in competition festivals; they regarded this as just as worth while and exciting as archery-matches or fencing-contests.

Wagner has used one of these contests in his opera *Tannhäuser*.

The troubadours and Minnesingers began to lose interest in this pastime during the 1200's, but for two hundred years they filled Europe with song. We, in England, had perhaps the most famous troubadour of all— King Richard Lion-heart. You will remember how, according to legend, he was helped to escape from prison in Austria, during the Crusades, by his favourite minstrel, Blondel.

In Germany, after the aristocracy lost interest this type of music was taken up by tradesmen and working men. Cobblers, bakers, tailors, butchers, all began to form themselves into clubs, or *guilds*, and, like the knights before them, held friendly singing contests. As they won, they went to a higher and higher grade until they at last became Mastersingers. Here again, Wagner has given us a wonderful picture of their activities in his opera *The Mastersingers*. It was after 1600 before the guilds of Mastersingers began finally to disappear, and they did so because they had surrounded their singing with so many stupid rules and customs that it gradually withered.

Meanwhile part-singing in the churches was growing more and more elaborate and beautiful. In England, France, Italy, and the Netherlands composers were experimenting with harmonies, rhythms, and sound-effects, and were learning to write them down in those musical symbols (semibreves, minims, crotchets) which we know so well. In fact, by about 1550 they were beginning to overreach themselves. They were so engrossed with the lovely, complicated music they were writing that they tended to forget about the meaning of the words—the hymns, psalms, and prayers of the church services. There was so much elaborate music going on that people in the congregations could not make out the words at all. Even worse, the composers were quite in the habit of borrowing good tunes from somewhere else to weave into their own music, and these tunes were often not at all the right ones to sing in church. Imagine listening to your church choir singing a sacred anthem in church one Sunday morning, with all the tenors singing *Tipperary* or "Roll out the barrel" in the middle of it! The Pope, worried about all this, set up a council of church dignitaries to see that church composers provided their churches with much simpler and more reverent music. This council, called the Council of Trent (1562), did its job so well that for a time it looked as if complicated part-singing in church services had come to a stop altogether.

At this point, however, something occurred which, as is so often the case in the history of any sort of art, made quite wonderfully sure that the right sort of church music should be preserved for ever. Growing up in Italy was a young composer who, in learning his job, was able to take in all the best aspects of the work of composers before him and was already producing church music more reverent, more noble, and more *pure* in style than any that had previously been heard. He was called Giovanni, but he will always be known by the name of the little town where he was born—Palestrina.

PAUSE

We have now arrived on the first peak in the landscape of European music, and we have got there so quickly that there has not been time to note several names and dates which are landmarks on the way. Here they are:

Early Christian Church Music

A.D.

600   Pope Gregory the First got some sort of order into the sung parts of the church service, by defining which modes were to be used, and what portions of the service were to be sung. A start had been made on this about 200 years earlier by Ambrose, Bishop of Milan.

900   Hucbald, a Flemish monk, laid down some of the first rules for part-singing, now gradually taking the place of plain-song.

1000   Guido d'Arezzo, also a monk, worked out systems of writing down music and of teaching people how to sing it at sight.

Troubadours and Minnesingers (1100–1300)

1250   Adam de la Halle is remembered as a famous *trouvère* because some of his music was so good that it was published as late as 1872. Among his works is a play, *The Play of Robin and Marion*, which consists of spoken parts and songs, like the Gilbert and Sullivan operas.

Church Music (1200–1500)

1300 John of Fornsete, a clerk of accounts at Reading Abbey, *wrote out* the famous round *Sumer is icumen in,* though he may not necessarily have composed it. The original manuscript dates from about 1226.

1400 John Dunstable was writing such good polyphonic music for church services that his music crossed over the sea to France and Italy.

1500 Josquin des Prés, of the Netherlands, served at the Vatican in Rome, and, with his northern talent, brought freshness and further beauty to Italian church music.

These dates given here are not the birth-dates or the death-dates of these old musicians; they merely indicate the period when they were doing most of their work.

4

Music emerges from the Twilight

YOU can go to concerts every day for a whole year and not hear a single note of Palestrina's music. He still lies outside the boundaries of the well-known, popular two hundred years of music which, for the most part, we continue to hear.

But if we are going to think about history at all we must often forget about the things that interest us in the present and try to imagine the things that must have caused an enormous stir among people (just like us) at an earlier time. When we open our newspapers we are very interested indeed to see what Queen Elizabeth II was doing yesterday; if, however, there was a feature-article on what Queen Elizabeth I did four hundred years ago we might skim over it. Yet that does not mean that one queen is greater or lesser than another.

When you are told in a book that one composer or another was great, or miraculous, or that he wrote music which was like the peak of a mountain, it does not mean that you may enjoy listening to his music any more than you might enjoy Queen Elizabeth I's views on Mary Queen of Scots. All the composer and the queen have in common is a historical interest. What Queen Elizabeth I said about affairs of State when she was on the throne has often guided the government of the country since those days. In the same way the music of Palestrina and his contemporaries has shown hundreds of later people how to write their own music—*because* those older musicians were such complete masters of their craft. Their music was not like Beethoven's, or Chopin's, Tchaikovsky's; it was written in a language that sounds as ancient to us as Chaucer's does, but, like Chaucer, it has its own arresting beauty, even for us in the twentieth century.

When we hear Palestrina's music, written to fill enormous churches with grave, celestial sound, we are likely to picture a humble monk, sitting in his grey stone cell, his eyes fixed on Eternity, and writing pages and pages of semibreves, minims, and Latin words until it was time to eat a frugal supper and lie down on a hard, cold bed. This was not the truth at all. Palestrina came from a well-to-do land-owning family; he began scribbling music when he was still a boy, and signed it "Giannetto" (Johnny). He was married twice—first at twenty-two and then later to a rich widow, who helped to pay for the publication of his music.

He was in the service of the Church for most of his life. After some years as organist and choirmaster in the cathedral of his native town Palestrina was given a choirmaster's appointment in Rome in 1551. In Rome his music could constantly reach the ears of the principal churchmen of the Vatican. He made quite sure he was noticed by the right people, as was the custom in any artistic circles in those days; he produced works "in gratitude for my appointment," "for His Holiness, who encourages music so much," or "in memory of . . .," when some important figure died. At the same time he would point out what a great deal of care he had taken to make the music worthy of the occasion.

Perhaps the one setback in his busy professional life was the rule made by a later Pope, Paul IV (when the composer was about thirty), that one of Palestrina's appointments must not be held by a married man. He was, however, pensioned off with an annual sum equal to what his salary had been, so that he lost nothing but official importance, and merely carried on his work in another church in the neighbourhood. During the twenty years that followed the Church's law-givers came and went; rules were cancelled and remade. In 1571 Palestrina

found his way back to the centre of church music: St
Peter's, Rome.

At the age of sixty-eight Palestrina died, leaving a huge
bulk of music of all kinds: masses, hymns, part-songs,
madrigals—all more beautiful and more advanced than
any music that had been heard before. When, on entering
a cathedral, we hear the choir singing Palestrina's church
music, we feel that the sound is a part of the building;
the lines of melody trace sometimes simple, sometimes
lavishly ornamental patterns for our ears as do those of
the stonework for our eyes; the firm, gravely beautiful,
gently-progressing harmonies seem, like the erect pillars
and the pointed arches, to rise straight to God. Music and
masonry melt and dissolve into each other to form the
perfect background to worship.

It was Palestrina's destiny to be able to sum up all the
attempts at church music that had been made before
him: to digest them, learn from them, and carry out what
the earlier composers had been trying, not always successfully, to achieve. That is his importance to the student
of musical history. To most listeners he is still the first
composer to bring music out into the broad light of to-day:
we *respond* to it; we can enjoy and understand the sound
of it.

Every student of musical composition must be able to
write music in the style of Palestrina; from this he learns
the discipline of creating beautiful effects (using the bare
minimum of notes) and the way to write *pure* music, with
no turn of tune or harmony which will sound cheap,
vulgar, or otherwise unsuitable.

The Council of Trent (which was mentioned earlier) set
up an inquiry into the state of church music, and, though
the investigators were bent on stamping out all elaborate
music (after the vulgarity of some composers had gone
too far), they laid no hands on Palestrina. It is not quite
true to say that his music was held up as an example of
the style others must follow, nor is it true (as some writers
insist) that the mass written in memory of Marcellus (Pope

Marcellus II) was made the pattern of all future masses. These are legends without any support in fact. What is important is that even this stern inquiry could not find fault with Palestrina, and he continued to enrich the art of music as it had never been enriched before.

If there is any quality in which Palestrina's music is wanting it is that of variety. Though he did not write church music all the time—he found time also to write madrigals, songs, and even a few comic duets—all the music has the same pure, angelic quality. It seemed as if he could not be funny, or romantic, or vulgar at any price. His musical paint-box did not include many colours, but it is all the more to his credit that he could paint such rare and beautiful pictures with them.

Having levelled this tiny criticism at Palestrina, it is time to introduce another composer, a 'twin' of Palestrina (they both died in 1594), and an equally important one to those who wish to find out how music grew. This is a Flemish composer, Orlandus Lassus, or Orlando di Lasso, who was born at Mons and who died at Munich. Let us call him Orlando. Orlando's church music aimed at the same ideals of reverence and purity as that of Palestrina; both composers can be heard in cathedrals in more or less equal proportions nowadays. There is one direction, however, in which Orlando pushed the growth of music a good deal farther than Palestrina. One of Orlando's posts was that of director of an orchestra, which was an experience Palestrina never had; Orlando therefore took special notice of the qualities and capabilities of musical instruments, as well as of voices. Though it is unlikely that he wrote music specifically for the orchestra there is no doubt that he had the sound of the orchestra, as well as that of the choir, in his mind when he wrote his choral music. Indeed, some of it is marked *buone da cantare e suonare* ("suitable for singing and playing").

He must have been an impressive man. Some one wrote that, as a choirmaster, "He gave the time with such steadiness, that like warriors at the sound of the trumpet, the expert singers needed no other orders than the expression of that powerful and vigorous countenance to animate their sweetly-sounding voices." Orlando travelled all his life; Palestrina stayed at home. Orlando wrote all sorts of music—serious, funny, popular, refined; Palestrina kept to his grave, celestial style. Orlando's music was a patchwork; Palestrina's was uniformly satisfying and uplifting. Orlando painted his pictures from a palette of rich, varied, jumbled colours; Palestrina used a few colours sparingly, but with the most beautiful effect always.

We must not leave this great period of church music without including one more composer—a Spaniard this time. His name was Tomás Luis de Victoria, and he was just a little younger than Palestrina and Orlando. Sixteen years of his career were spent in Rome, and he knew both these composers; in fact there is no doubt that he and Palestrina learned quite a lot from each other of the ways of writing church music. Victoria's music is all serious, sacred, and somewhat mysterious. It is also simpler on the whole than that of the other two. He did not write such flowing, interweaving tunes as the others did but relied a good deal more on upright chords (as we get in the hymns we sing every day) to achieve his effects. One of his most beautiful little anthems could be sung by any school choir which can raise treble, alto, tenor, and bass voices; it is called "Jesu, the very thought is sweet." The choir will find it simple, very singable, and most satisfying to work at and perform. Easier than Palestrina or Orlando, it is just as good music, and is typical of their styles of writing. It was just that kind of music which was enriching and beautifying the church services all over Europe.

Palestrina was an Italian, Orlando di Lasso a Fleming, and Victoria a Spaniard. It must seem so far that music had settled down to live on the Continent, centred in

Rome, far away from this fog-bound little northern island upon which we live. This certainly did happen in the 1500's; the centre of the art of music moved southward, like a heat-wave, to Italy—but it moved from the north, from England. It is true that, four hundred years ago, a bright young music student, needing first-rate lessons, would feel he had to go to Rome to find the best teachers and to listen to the greatest music. Six hundred years ago, however, he would have found his way to the South of England, to the great, bustling Abbey at Reading, or to a church in London where he would find John Dunstable, the man whose music, well-known in Rome, showed Palestrina the way. Here, and only here, could he learn how to combine several parts, how to set Latin words so as to bring out their deepest meaning, and how to play the organ really well.

And now, as the 1500's were drawing to a close, music was moving on again. There is no doubt that, with the deaths of Palestrina, Orlando, and Victoria, the face of Continental music was changing. The air was alive with experiment and restlessness. Composers were becoming weary of the interwoven, many-tuned church music; in any case it had been done so perfectly that the younger composers had the depressing feeling that anything they wrote could not possibly be as good. Like a rich vein of ore, it had been worked out; a new one must be found and explored.

The first moves were made in two directions: towards secular (*i.e.*, non-sacred) music, and towards stage music. The former produced the lighthearted, expressive part-songs which we know as *madrigals*, and the latter led to *opera*. But more about the latter development in the next chapter. What is important now is to welcome music's centre back to our own shores, where Henry VIII, himself a composer, was reigning.

Of course music had not 'stopped' in England since the great days of John Dunstable and his fellows. There had always been a steady flow of it in cathedrals and churches, and it had been growing in richness and variety just as it had been in Europe. But, as we have seen, the summit of excellence rose above Rome; we in England were near it, but still on the slopes. It was just when Rome, tiring of polyphonic music (let us call it now by its usual name), began to 'go back to school again' and learn new ways of composition, that England produced a large clump of composers who drew the centre of music's excellence back to this country.

Of these, let us concentrate on two of the most important, whose music you can hear and sing most often. They are Thomas Tallis and William Byrd. Tallis lived and died in the 1500's, and Byrd, a younger man, lived over the turn of the century until 1623. They were lifelong friends, and both made their music as members of the Chapel Royal, which was not a building but a gathering of musicians and priests attached to the Royal Household to provide music and services of worship for the reigning monarch. (During one of his French campaigns, in 1418, Henry the Fifth sent for his Chapel Royal to help celebrate Easter at Bayeux.)

During Tallis's lifetime, and eight years before Byrd was born, a most important historical event occurred. King Henry VIII, who was on the throne, declared that "the Bishop of Rome hath no jurisdiction in this realm and Empire of England." In other words the Catholic Church, the cradle of music during all those centuries, was to cease to exist here. In its place was to be a church formed by Henry and his Archbishops—the Church of England. The monasteries, the seats of musical activities and tuition, were to be done away with, and all religious services were to be said and sung in English instead of in Latin. This Reformation of the churches could obviously not be carried out without a good deal of strife and unrest. Priests were burnt at the stake if they refused to make the change; many great musicians lost their posts when the abbeys and monasteries were closed down; some of them narrowly escaped martyrdom in the early stages of the Reformation through persisting in setting Latin words for the church services. In fact, in the case of some of them, it was only because Henry—and, later, Elizabeth—were keen musicians themselves that they were treated a good deal more tenderly than were the priests under whom they served. In short, the entire firm, solid background of the Church, against which so many great musicians had worked throughout the centuries, was knocked away and dissolved round them.

It is interesting to see how, with typical English habits of compromise, Tallis and Byrd continued to write their vocal music sometimes in English and sometimes in the frowned-on language of Latin. They must have felt that only the excellence of their music and their usefulness to English music stood between them and imprisonment, or worse. In fact we know of only one composer of that time, John Taverner, who publicly said he was sorry he had written so many "Popish ditties," and sank himself in the ways of the new reformed Church.

Nevertheless, the music of Tallis and Byrd does show some very interesting points of difference from that of Palestrina and Orlando—differences which might be the effect of their being Catholics 'on the run' from authority. Where the Italians wrote spacious music, with broad effects suitable for large, open services in the heart of the Catholic religion, the Englishmen often wrote on a smaller scale. Many of their striking effects—their exquisite clashings of notes, their delicate accentuation of important words—are almost lost in big performances in enormous churches. Could it be that they were meant to be sung in back rooms, in hidden small buildings, out of earshot of the new Protestants? It might well be so.

Tallis and Byrd were excellent craftsmen. They had the priceless gift of being able to manipulate the various strands of their polyphonic writing so that, besides being ingenious, it sounded beautiful and was exciting to sing. Many of you must have sung two very simple but lovely pieces of music by Tallis and Byrd. Tallis's tune to the hymn "Glory to Thee, my God, this night," is a wonderful piece of musical mechanism; it is expressive and dignified, and it can be sung in four parts at once with very little practice. As soon as singer 1 has sung "Glory to Thee" singer 2 begins to sing the tune; when he gets to the same place singer 3 begins, and lastly, at the same place, singer 4. This kind of composition is known as a *canon*, and this hymn-tune is called (as you will see at the top of your hymn-book) Tallis's Canon. There is also a canon by Byrd (or often attributed to him) which is often sung in schools as a grace before a meal. This is in Latin—"Non nobis, Domine, non nobis; sed nomini tuo da gloriam." ("Not unto us, O Lord, not unto us; but to Thy Name give glory.") This is a little more complicated than Tallis's Canon. It is for three voices; when the first voice has sung the first word, "Non," the second voice begins the tune *four notes lower*; then the third voice comes in an octave lower than the first voice. These are simple examples of composers' work which, of course, included much more elaborate and magnificent music; they contain, however, a spirit of devotion which is just as inspiring to us in the twentieth century as it was in the sixteenth.

The 1500's came to an end, and England had the head-quarters of music firmly established in its midst; but Italy had yet another form of music-making to export to us. In 1588 there appeared in England a book of part-songs called *Musica Transalpina* ("Music from Across the Alps"). These were not sacred songs. They were in the polyphonic style, but their words (translated into English from *Italian*, not Latin) dealt with lighthearted situations and affairs, with many a 'girl-meets-boy' story—humorous, wistful, merry, and gently sad. This collection of songs came into the hands of one of the singing-men in St Paul's Cathedral Choir. He lived near by in a house in the City, and gathered together a small crowd of local gentlemen of leisure, businessmen, doctors, and lawyers to try these part-songs over. This meeting in the little parlour of the chorister's house became a regular one; it also set a fashion. From that day to this small groups of singers throughout the whole country have been meeting regularly to sing through the hundreds of delicious part-songs of this type, which are still called by their Italian name: madrigals.

To be able to sing a part in a madrigal was just as important for an Elizabethan gentleman as to be able to ride a horse, dance, wield a sword of fencing-stick, and be gallant to a lady. After a good supper our host and hostess brought out, not the bridge or canasta sets, but the madrigal books, and there around the table the company raised their voices in song. Madrigal-singing became in a very short time the fashionable thing to do throughout middle-class and aristocratic society.

As the habit grew, the great composers of the day settled down joyfully to write more and more madrigals to meet the demand, with the result that in a mere thirty years (1590–1620) such a store of excellent madrigals was built up as will give any enthusiast sufficient material to last his whole lifetime.

It was extremely fortunate, too, that some of the finest poetry in the English language was being written at this time. Though very few of the Elizabethan poets have signed the words of their madrigal verses, it is certain that most of the famous ones must have been hard at work producing the joyous, delicate, picturesque words which fit hand-in-glove with the music. Often the words did not *mean* anything much; there was a great deal of fa-la-la-ing, tuwhit-tuwhoo-ing, and hey-nonny-nonny-ing, and such first lines as "Down the hills Corinna trips," "Simkin said that Sis was fair," "Mother, I will have a husband." But, like short stories, madrigals could crystallize in a few bars of music a multitude of moods and fancies; words and music together could reach right to the nerve-centre of all sorts of fleeting fancies that pass through the minds of people.

Madrigals were written in any number of parts, from two to seven or eight, but there was usually only one singer per part. Often, too, all the parts were in one book, so that the singers had to crowd round, sit close together, and look over shoulders. They are *intimate* music, not meant to be sung by large choirs with a conductor, nor did they need large, well-trained voices. They are not for the concert hall; they are 'room-music.'

The list of madrigal composers is a long and exhausting one, and has no place here. There are so many of them, and all are so remarkable that any one of them would have been an important historical figure at this wonderful time in the development of music in England. It must suffice to mention only two: Thomas Morley and Orlando Gibbons. These represent not only the beginning and end of the madrigal period, but two opposite poles of musical style. Between Morley's *Now is the Month of Maying* and Gibbons's *The Silver Swan* lies the whole world of madrigal moods: Morley's, with its fa-la refrain, seems almost to have been written to dance to; Gibbons's, unutterably pathetic and melancholy, is the heartbreaking cry of a man for whom the world has become too frivolous and unkind:

> Farewell all joys; now Death, come close mine eyes;
> More geese than swans now live, more fools than wise.

Gather together five or six friends who can read music, give out the copies of these two madrigals, find a suitable starting-note on a recorder, or by getting some one to whistle it, and grope your way through them, sitting round a table or perching on your classroom desks. You will not rest until you have explored the entire intervening madrigal world.

Music, it was said in an earlier chapter, is a matter of either singing or playing (or both together, of course). It must seem so far that all music since the days of the ancient Jewish Church must have been sung music. What has happened to the playing of it? Of course, instrumental music was going on all the time: organs were

being played in churches; the troubadours and Minnesingers probably sang to an instrumental accompaniment;
many noble houses all over Europe kept large gatherings
of players (we cannot use the term 'orchestra' yet) to
make festive music on important occasions; lots of the
large churches had their services accompanied by
recorders, harps, trombones, trumpets, flutes. The English
madrigals themselves could be played as well as sung,
and we may suppose that often some singer, delayed on
his way to a madrigal party, must have had his part filled
in by an instrumental player.

The organ had a clear lead on all the other instruments;
even towards the end of the 1500's there were brilliant
players, such as Sweelinck, who drew enormous audiences
to hear their music: here began the concert habit.

In England, during the madrigal period, another keyboard instrument had found its way not into public halls
or churches, but into homes, where most of England's
music was made. This was the virginals, referred to in
Chapter 2. It was a favourite instrument of Queen Elizabeth I, who was quite an accomplished performer on it.
Music for the virginals was being written by many of the
madrigal composers. It must have been a most pleasant
change for them to be able to write music which was not
limited by the range of the voices, the speed of singing, or
the strict rules which church music had to obey. They
could enjoy themselves with all kinds of variations and
'twiddles' that singers could not manage. Their only
handicap (though they did not think of it as such) was
that they confined all their playing to the four fingers on
each hand; it just did not occur to them that they could
make it all a great deal easier by using their two thumbs
as well.

Virginals music seems to have been a kind of safety-
valve, a recreation, for the Elizabethan composers.
William Byrd, in the midst of writing his grave church
music and solemn madrigals, found time to compose *Mr
Byrd's Battle*, a piece of descriptive music which must

have been a great favourite, with its rattling, warlike noises; Tallis and Morley provided popular dance-tunes; Dr John Bull wrote variations on well-known comic songs of the time (*The King's Hunt, Watkins Ale*). Perhaps the most endearing virginals composer was Giles Farnaby, who has been described as "the Chopin of the Elizabethan Age." In his delicate, intimate little keyboard pieces (called by such names as *Giles Farnaby's Dreame, His Rest, His Humour*) can be found the same poetic grace that causes Chopin's music to speak so clearly and melodiously to us.

A picture gradually emerges, then, of an England full of amateur music-making, where singing and playing were social occupations just as natural and as important as golf, bridge, and dancing. One must realize, though, that madrigals and keyboard-playing were largely limited to the higher levels of society; music-making was not evenly spread over all classes of the community, any more than golf is in these days. It needed more money, education, and leisure time than the unskilled workers of the day could possibly give to it. We shall notice as we go on how this situation began to change, until, as at the present, amateur music was largely fostered and kept alive by working people.

To complete the picture of musical England under Queen Elizabeth I it remains to add two other forms of 'house music,' both instrumental. One was the *consort of viols*, which was a gathering of players instead of madrigal singers, and was the 'great-grandfather' of the string quartet we know so well nowadays. Viols were the ancestors of our violins, violas, cellos, and double-basses; but they were more complicated, had more strings, and were all played in the same manner as a cello (none were held under the chin). Englishmen must have been very good at playing viols, and it is pleasant to find that musicians came here from Germany and Italy to learn how to play them. A great deal of beautiful music was written (by Byrd, Gibbons, Morley, and other composers) for groups of viols, and many of the madrigals were stated in the original editions to be "apt for voices or viols." A musical evening could be a very varied affair; we can imagine the after-supper singers saying, "That was a fine madrigal. Let's get the viols out and hear what it sounds like on them!"

Finally there was the lute, an indispensable part of a gentleman's social equipment. This portable, pear-shaped instrument had a very long life. It was used in the beginnings of music, and was probably kept in mind by Schubert, only 150 years ago, when he wrote a part for the guitar (it is sometimes played on a lute) in a string quartet. The player plucked the strings and sang to its accompaniment. Barber's shops used to have one hanging on the wall for the use of customers while they were waiting for a vacant chair. From all accounts it was an expensive instrument to keep up; one nobleman of the time said that he could keep a horse for a year on the money his lute cost him in new strings!

John Dowland and Thomas Campion are the names to remember among the lutenist composers. With such songs as Dowland's *Flow not so fast, ye fountains*, and Campion's *Shall I come, sweet love, to thee?* music finally comes out of the shadows.

This hundred years, from 1500 to 1600, has seen the art of music growing fast, shifting from place to place in importance, and—most important of all—producing songs, madrigals, church music, and instrumental music that we, in the twentieth century, can sing, play, and listen to with enjoyment. Let us think of a spotlight, playing over the musical scene in the 1500's and picking out the hills and hollows of the path along which music has journeyed. Sweeping first to the point in time farthest away from us, it illuminates a fairly steep gradient sloping up from a shadowy lowland, upon which can be discerned the figures of church musicians in England, France, the Netherlands, Germany, and Italy, all experimenting in the writing down of music, the effective setting of words, and the manipulating of the notes to produce richer and nobler effects. As the beam moves slowly towards us the summit of the slope comes sharply into focus; it is situated in Rome, and upon it are the great polyphonists—Palestrina, di Lasso, Victoria. But already the light is moving on (the Italians are beginning to grope towards different music, and having to experiment with it) and is coming northward towards England, lifting out of the shadows several stretches of upland in Germany and the Netherlands, and resting on the highest peak of all, London and the Chapel Royal. On this broad summit are Tallis, Byrd, Morley, Gibbons, Farnaby, John Bull, and, as an enthusiastic patron and performer, Queen Elizabeth I herself.

There are no sudden changes in direction in the history of an art; each generation tries to carry forward what the preceding one has been trying to do. Church music was developing steadily in England while all eyes were turned to Rome; madrigals were flourishing in Italy before they became the fashion in England and were brought to a new pitch of excellence. It is when it happens that—in music—composers, performers, patrons, and an enthusiastic *feeling* for the art all gather together in the same place that the light of history becomes focused on it for a time.

But again the focus was shifting. The language of music was changing; it was moving out from the confines of the Church and of the home. England, rent with political troubles and civil war in the middle 1600's, was no longer the place in which an art could develop; experiments on the Continent in new forms of music had been going steadily on since Palestrina's time. The spotlight of musical history moved southward again to its previous resting-place—Italy.

PAUSE

Here are some more landmarks, and a summary of events between Palestrina and the end of the great English Madrigal period:

The Italians

Palestrina (1525–94)

Lassus (1530–94). Flemish by birth, but made music in Rome, and belonged to that school.

Victoria (1535–1611). A Spaniard who also regarded Rome as his musical spiritual home.

In the case of all three composers their dates of birth are only approximate.

1563 The commission set up by the Council of Trent found fault with the elaborateness and lack of reverence of much of the church music, and recommended ways of simplifying and improving it.

The English

1509 Henry VIII came to the throne. An amateur composer and player, he looked charitably on musical activities. In reforming the Church and establishing the Church of England, causing English to take the place of Latin, he did, however, cause considerable anxiety among church composers who, however Catholic or Protestant they were, had become used to writing settings of the Latin texts.

1558 Elizabeth I came to the throne. England entered on a Golden Age of music and poetry.

1550–1620 Principal composers:
             Vocal: Tallis, Byrd, Morley, Dowland, Wilbye,
             Weelkes, Campion, Gibbons.
             Instrumental: Byrd, Bull, Farnaby, Morley.

Important collections of music of this period:

A collection of twenty-nine madrigals written to honour Queen Elizabeth I. Twenty-six composers contributed to it. Each madrigal ended with the words:

"Thus sang the shepherds and nymphs of Diana,
Long live fair Oriana."

The collection was published, however, just a few months after "Oriana" (*i.e.*, Elizabeth) had died.

The *Fitzwilliam Virginal Book*. A collection of keyboard music by various composers, copied out by an enthusiastic virginals player in the early 1600's. From this collection we have learnt nearly all we know about the keyboard music of that time. It was given to Cambridge University by Viscount Fitzwilliam in 1816, and was published in the 1890's.

The Beginnings of Opera and the Rise of Instrumental Music

IN the middle 1500's a strong feeling was growing in Italy that music should stand more firmly on its own feet. After all, the whole object of all the fine church music was to provide a background for worship; it was, so to speak, a gorgeous backcloth or scenery against which the chief actors in the ritual of the Church moved and spoke. The time had come to link up music a good deal more closely with human affairs—human characters, moods, stories, situations—and to cause music to be an *expression* rather than merely a design. Music moved towards plays and stories, and the result was the 'new music': the twin forms of *opera* and *oratorio*.

While, in England, musicians were in the full flood of the madrigal era various experiments in opera were being carried out in Italy. In the year Palestrina died Orazio Vecchi produced a light comedy called *Amfiparnasso*, written in the form of a series of madrigals, with music of varying moods to fit the various characters, of which there were five. They all sang all the time; if only two characters happened to be on the stage the other three sang behind the scenes to accompany them. There were no instruments. Six years later, in 1600, the opera *Euridyce*, written by Jacopo Peri, told that most famous of all classical stories with singers and a few instruments to accompany them. This can safely be thought of as the first true opera, the forerunner of all operas as we know them now.

In the same year, curiously enough, another composer

was experimenting with a dramatic setting of a sacred story. In Rome Emilio di Cavalieri had produced a sacred drama called *The Representation of Soul and Body*, in which the characters were *ideas* rather than people; they represented such ideas as Time, Life, Intellect, and Soul. There was a certain amount of costume and acting, and even some sacred dancing, but the work was meant for devout performance in church, in the manner of our Nativity plays. Here, however, was the beginning of oratorio, which was soon to lead to the *St Matthew Passion* and *Messiah*, and, later, to *Elijah*, and *The Dream of Gerontius*.

As time went on there was more and more action and movement in opera, and less and less in oratorio, until opera came to be spoken of as "oratorio on wheels," and oratorio as "frozen opera!"

Music was beginning to 'show off' on the stage. It was also coming out from the shelter of private houses, and being dragged into public places by 'star' performers. Keyboard instruments and lutes were developing in size and were easier to play; composers were writing more difficult and showy music; players were practising hard to play it. Great organists, like Frescobaldi, Sweelinck, Froberger, and Dr Bull, were drawing audiences of thousands to listen to them. After a hundred years of hard struggle the most essential orchestral instrument, the violin, was beginning to be accepted, though the players of lutes and viols still disliked it for its harsh shrillness. Music as a means of public display had begun to be exploited; with the star performer singing and playing to an audience the public concert was born.

At this point it will be most useful to look over the whole scene of Europe's music during the seventeenth century. The art was developing so widely and rapidly that it is no longer possible to allow the beam of history to focus itself on any one place. We will therefore see what was happening in the various countries, and try to place the important events in some sort of order.

Italy

The early experiments in opera were being followed up by the first master of the art—Claudio Monteverde. Always anxious to try out new ways of making music, Monteverde greatly enriched the orchestral accompaniments to the singers, making the instruments enhance the moods of the music with their special tone-colours. For instance, he was one of the first composers to use the despised violins, and certainly the first to find out that if the bow was pushed and pulled rapidly over the strings they gave out a very effective rustling, trembling sound— a picturesque background to the singers.

It is unfortunate, however, that after this fine start opera began to go wrong. The most important people in any opera are the singers. It is they who portray the characters and the drama through their voices; it is to them that an opera chiefly owes its effect. It is not surprising that all the other indispensable people—the composer, the stage manager, the scenic artist, the instrumentalists—found themselves taken for granted. The singers were supreme, and they knew they were. The audiences went to hear them, and it was their duty to show off as much as possible. So they would hold up the entire show while they shrieked and carolled, making every song into an orgy of scales, runs, and 'twiddles.' Though it is unbelievable, it is a fact that an audience applauded for five minutes after the *first note* sung by one of these petted darlings. The main offenders were the unnatural 'male sopranos,' men whose boyish voices were preserved by artificial means during their adult lives. Plump, pompous, and pampered, they were the equivalent of those young men who are billed as "singers" at the variety theatres nowadays, and who can cause swooning in the galleries and riots at the stage door. One of these *castrati*, as they were called, made sufficient money in England to build himself a palace in Italy, which he called, cynically, "England's Folly." If the public liked that sort of thing so much it was obvious that composers would have to write music that would fit in with it. The result was a spate of operas with hardly any story, no characterization at all, and lots of songs, often superficially brilliant, which the star singers could use as a means of displaying their vulgar talents.

Only a few composers stood out against this deplorable fashion, such as Alessandro Scarlatti, a learned teacher as well as a composer, who clung dauntlessly to the pure operatic syle of Monteverde.

(Alessandro's son, Domenico Scarlatti, who lived for some time in Spain, is famous for different reasons: he made sweeter music out of the harpsichord than had ever been heard before. His works for this instrument opened up a new age of splendid, dazzling keyboard-playing.)

France

Stage music appealed to the French people more than home music or church music. Opera was first properly established in France by an Italian: Giovanni Battiste Lully. Although he was taken to France when he was about twelve years old, he had been a very gifted child, and had known just what was going on in the exciting operatic world of 'new music' in his native country. Soon he was appointed a violinist in the private orchestra (the 'twenty-four violins') of King Louis XIV, then a boy of about fifteen, and from that time onward he was undisputed king of music in France. His main contribution to opera is his musical treatment of the 'talking-bits'; if one or two characters had some dialogue to get through, they used at first to sing it in a half-talking manner, with just a few chords on the harpsichord to make it sound like music. Lully made these dialogue passages yet more musical by developing the new idea of having them accompanied by the orchestra, just like the popular tunes in the opera. The Italian method was called *recitativo secco*, or 'dry recitative'; Lully's was called *recitativo stromentato*, or 'accompanied recitative.' Lully was able to write a first-rate tune, dignified and free from Italian 'twiddles'; and he brought opera to a greatly higher standard than it had ever attained before. He was a disagreeable person and a brutal businessman, jealous and unscrupulous. By a series of furtive tricks he managed to grasp all the threads of Paris musical life; at one time no theatre in Paris was allowed to have more than half the orchestra he employed at the opera. He died in 1687 through hitting his toe with the rod which he used to beat out the time on the floor!

England

It is not quite as simple as it seems to account for the decline in English music after the great Elizabethan period. A glory had certainly departed, and the blame could easily be placed on the shoulders of the Puritans, were it not that Cromwell and the great poet Milton were keen and sympathetic musicians. What the Puritans did do was to stand in the way of musical progress by frowning so heavily on stage performances; the 'new music' of the opera and the play was kept away from these shores for too long. Also, a stormy era in which a civil war raged, a king was beheaded, a commonwealth was declared, and the monarchy was restored (all between 1640 and 1660) was not the most favourable one in which music could flourish as it did in the previous, more settled age.

Until the Restoration (1660) English music was in the keeping of harmless, conventional church musicians, and distinguished writers of delicate songs in the manner of Dowland and Campion. One of these, Henry Lawes, wrote music for Milton's *Comus*. As if at a signal, however, the Restoration unleashed the art of music again through musicians who had been quietly growing up and learning throughout the Commonwealth, and through one, the greatest of them all, who was born a year or so before King Charles II's return.

First there was Matthew Locke, a chorister of Exeter Cathedral (he once carved his name in the stone of the organ-screen when nobody was looking) who wrote the music for the procession of Charles II through London in 1661, on the day before his Coronation. There was the boy-prodigy, Pelham Humfrey, who had written such fine church music by the age of seventeen that he was sent by King Charles to study in France with Lully. Tragically, he died when he was only twenty-seven.

Shortly before the Restoration, however, (in 1658 or 1659) was born one of England's most distinguished and dearly loved composers; one whose music continues to be the staple diet of solo singers and church choirs. Henry Purcell deserves a higher place in this book than one of the 'Signpost' chapters. His music is more beautiful and advanced than that of any other composer mentioned in them. The fact remains, however, that for all his excellence he was a 'flash in the pan,' a happy interlude along the path of history. He began his life as a chorister in the Chapel Royal, where he is certain to have met Pelham Humfrey, fresh from his studies of the 'new music' in Paris. We know little about him, and what we do know is disputed over and over again by one scholar after another. What we do possess is his music—a superb collection of anthems, sets of incidental music for plays, some works for strings, songs, harpsichord music, and, most important, some operas. *Dido and Aeneas* was, however, Purcell's only opera in the modern sense of the word. Such works as *King Arthur* and *The Fairy Queen*, though described as operas at the time they were written, are in fact mixtures of stage-play, ballet, and song.

As a Court musician Purcell would have ample opportunity of getting to know the work of Italian and French composers, and (being the great composer he was) of improving on them. This he did, especially in the instrumental music (two violinists and a pianist can revel in the 'Golden Sonata'), and in the 'operas,' notably *Dido and Aeneas*, written for a girls' school. This opera (which contains 'Dido's Lament,' one of the most moving songs in the world) shows us by its very artistry and feeling just how far the Italians had strayed from the orginal

MUSIC AT A ROYAL COURT IN BACH'S TIME

A. Menzel

The King himself (Frederick the Great) is playing a flute concerto with his orchestra, which is being directed by the harpsichordist.

"Picture Post" Library

MORNING PRAYER IN BACH'S HOME

T. E. Rosenthal

Some of Bach's children are taking part.

"Picture Post" Library

MOZART AT THE AGE OF EIGHT

Mozarteum, Salzburg

He "did not learn, but merely remembered."

"Picture Post" Library

SCHUBERT'S MUSIC IS HEARD BY HIS FRIENDS

Carl Roling

The composer is accompanying a singer during a performance of his own songs.

"Picture Post" Library

ideals of opera. The characters have music to sing which fits them, and no one is given the slightest chance to show off the voice in meaningless strings of notes. Purcell also had the ability to write a really fine and satisfying tune. There is a deep delight to be felt in the singing of "Fairest Isle" (from the 'opera' *King Arthur*), "I attempt from love's sickness to fly," or "Sound the Trumpet," with its two weaving, exulting voices. It is all the more remarkable that this last song, and also 'Dido's Lament' ("When I am laid in earth"), are anchored to what is known as a *ground bass*; the bass part, which you can hear played by the piano accompanist's left hand while you are singing, consists of a short tune constantly repeated. It is quite astonishing to hear Purcell writing his long, serene tunes on this monotonous 'left-hand' repeated tune; so cleverly is it done that one just does not notice the repetition in performance.

Much of Purcell's music was written for special occasions—the Queen's birthdays, the anniversaries of St Cecilia (patron saint of music), and royal marriages. He must have been hard put to it to produce suitable music all the time, as was the duty of a Court composer, and it is a wonder that there is so little dull music among what he wrote.

Purcell had a short life; in 1695 he died and was buried in Westminster Abbey, as befits a true immortal. In spite of the fine work he put into *Dido and Aeneas* and his other stage works, he did not succeed in founding a style that would be copied later; nor did he advance the great work of writing music for the keyboard, his harpsichord suites being slight works. If he passed anything on to help history on its way it was the ability to write music which would sound large and splendid when sung by huge choruses. There is no doubt that, a mere forty years later, a composer was showing that he had learned a lot from Purcell about choral music—George Frederick Handel.

Germany

Our grandfathers and our great-grandfathers went to Germany as a matter of course to learn how to be musicians. Germany for us is perhaps still the fount of music—for us who are reared on Mozart, Haydn, Beethoven, and Schubert. In fact, it was the Germans who described England as "a land without music," and said of its composers, "English composers, no composers at all." So far we have hardly mentioned them; they do not seem to have had the spotlight on them for more than a passing moment. What was happening to them all this time? How did they soon become the centre of music?

Music in Germany was, of course, going on, developing steadily, just as it was doing in Italy, France, and England. Its growth was mainly in church music. The rot that had set in in Italy, through using music as a means of displaying the powers of pampered soloists, had not yet attacked German musicians; they were serious-minded, devout, and (let it be said) not too anxious to make changes. Heinrich Schütz (who died in 1672, aged eighty-seven) had brought oratorio to its highest peak so far by setting the story of Christ's death to music; Buxtehude's organ-playing in Lübeck drew crowds of students and listeners—including the young Bach, who walked two hundred miles to hear him. The town bands, a popular feature of the German musical scene, were the cradle of many excellent wind-instrument players. All was proceeding quietly forward to ensure that the focus would very soon be on Germany.

In 1685 Bach and Handel were born.

5

Bach and Handel

AT this point we can (without being too inaccurate) regard the flow of musical history as a river. Ignoring for the moment the Jewish and Greek music, we can see this river appearing as a strong, single stream, emerging from under the ground some six hundred years ago—a stream of church music. On it flowed, becoming ever wider and deeper, until at the end of the 1500's it began to spread out into a delta, with several rivers proceeding in different directions: church music, stage music, orchestral music, music for the solo singer, and the solo player. When a river does that it usually means it is near the sea.

You may ask why a musical river should find its goal in this way. Can there be a musical sea? There is, in the shape of a composer who was able not only to absorb all the finest elements in music of earlier times but to 'step them all up' to a higher and richer degree of excellence. There is hardly a single musician these days who does not acknowledge him without hesitation as the greatest musician of all time.

He was a hard-working, ill-paid local organist and teacher. He spent his days training his choir, writing music for them to sing, and playing the organ at services; he never travelled abroad and, except as a brilliant organist, he had no great fame beyond the city of Leipzig, where he spent most of his life. His name was Johann Sebastian Bach.

His name means 'brook,' but his musical genius was in fact as wide and as deep as the sea. Just as rivers reach their destination in the sea, so did all the various kinds of music flow into Bach's mind and spirit, there to be made richer and more full of feeling than they had ever been. Even a simple hymn-tune, when Bach had done with it, would blossom forth in new and more beautiful sound. In *The Oxford Book of Carols* you will find the well-known carol *In dulci jubilo* in two forms; one was harmonized by some one about a hundred years before Bach, and the other by Bach himself. Both are good; but notice the difference between them, especially in the bass parts. Bach's bass is hardly ever still: it ranges right from the highest notes to the lowest ones, and moves in quick notes and slow ones; in fact, it is an exciting and melodious tune all by itself. So are the alto and tenor parts. The important point about this adventurous writing is that it does not make the hymn sound complicated or flowery; in fact it causes it to sound more beautiful, and makes us feel its mood more vividly and deeply.

If a film-director were to try and make a film of Bach's life he would find it very difficult. Nothing startling or romantic ever happened to Bach. There were no journeys overseas, or brilliant concerts in foreign cities; the public did not mob him, nor did he ever become a glamorous celebrity. The only milestones along the path of his life are the various jobs in which he found himself; but these are important, as they caused him to write various sorts of music. To begin with, it would have been strange if he had not been a musician, as the male members of the Bach family had nearly all been organists, singers, or bandsmen for nearly a hundred years before Johann Sebastian was born. He seems, however, to have had a thorough all-round education, right until he was fifteen, and until that time all the music he had was some lessons in keyboard-playing and some training for his very fine treble voice. Nothing could stop him from pressing forward with music, not even his elder brother's refusal to let him look at some new music he had brought into the house. The boy found where it was hidden, took it to his room, and stealthily copied it out by moonlight! After several small posts as church organist he arrived, at the age of twenty-three, in Weimar, where he was given charge of the music at the court of a local nobleman. Here, besides a very good small orchestra, was a larger and better organ than he had so far played. This instrument, spurring him on to write music for it, was that on which the greatest organ music in the world must have been played. Now it was that a musical river, that of organ music, found its destination in the sea; never before had such profound and beautiful music issued from the instrument as the Toccata and Fugue in D minor, the Chorale Preludes, and the great Passacaglia, in which the strong, vigorous bass notes march so splendidly over the pedal board.

At thirty-two he moved again, this time to another nobleman's court, at Cöthen, but with an orchestra to conduct instead of an organ to play. Here he wrote the violin concertos, the Brandenburg Concertos, the sonatas for flute and for violin, and other works for combinations of instruments which could be played in the drawing-room (as well as much keyboard music). Many of these are so enjoyable to play that those taking part in them smile happily at each other and say, "Let's play it all again" when they get to the end. It is the perfect 'music of friends,' and has such a soothing and invigorating effect on players and listeners that they can almost hear Bach saying to them, "Come now! There really isn't anything to worry about, you know!"

Six years later Bach left Cöthen and went to Leipzig as cantor (*i.e.*, musical director) of St Thomas's School, which supplied the city's churches with choirboys. He also directed the performance of the choir and orchestra in St Thomas's Church. Bach was to stay here until he died at the age of sixty-five. Besides giving singing instruction to the boys at the school, which he did on five mornings each week, he was obliged to write choral music for special services, university ceremonies, and city hall events. It was a busy life, and Bach was not long in finding how difficult it was to serve so many masters while keeping on friendly terms with them all. However, he poured out cantatas, oratorios, music for Easter and Christmas, and organ music until, in 1749, his eyesight gave way, and he died a year later.

People who do not know anything about music, but who like to think they do, are liable to call Bach "highbrow." They might even say that they "don't like Bach," and if you ask them why they say that his music "hasn't got a tune in it." In a sense they are right when they say this, because Bach's music rarely has one tune, it has two or three running along at the same time, with a strong, steady bass to bind them together. Here is an example:

Zi-on hears her watch-men's voi - ces

The cantata *Sleepers, Wake!*, by J. S. Bach

While the tenors of the choir sing a grave hymn-tune the violins are weaving a completely separate tune round them, and the deep instruments are walking solidly along, providing a foundation. Compare that with another type of music, a Mozart piano sonata:

There the tune is all that matters. The right hand plays it while the left hand merely plays a simple accompaniment. Your ear *listens* to the right-hand tune; it merely *overhears* the accompaniment in the left hand. You might like to think of Bach's way of writing like making a crossword puzzle. Your 'across' clues must make sensible words, and you can have as many as you like under each other, provided the 'down' clues make sensible words too. So Bach was able to write several long, flowing tunes, all singing along together, and all *harmonizing*; that is to say, all making sense from top to bottom as well as forward. A listener who is just used to listening to the 'tune on the top' naturally finds that he has to work a little harder when listening to Bach, but he soon realizes that Bach's music contains a good deal more than 'tune.' Far more striking is the extreme beauty and strength contained in the weaving together of several tunes:

The *Fugue in E*, from Book 2 of *The Forty-eight Preludes and Fugues*, by J. S. Bach

Sometimes, indeed, Bach quite deliberately writes music without a 'tune' in it, and in one case at least the 'tuneless' music has turned out to be one of the most popular of his keyboard pieces. The Prelude in C (from Book I of the Forty-eight Preludes and Fugues) delights our ear not with a tune, but with its meltingly beautiful succession of harmonies, each merging into the other:

Just as a fine painter can give us a picture consisting purely of soft, varying colours, and without any kind of figure, or house, or tree, so could Bach rely on mere changing harmonies to command all the attention we usually give to a warm, well-loved tune.

Bach has written music for nearly every one who can sing or play an instrument. Only the clarinet (which had hardly been invented in Bach's day) and the trombone (used very occasionally as a noise-maker) are left out. The pianist can begin with the delightful little dance-pieces in the *Anna Magdelena Music Book* (a collection of simple music that Bach wrote to help his wife to learn how to play the harpsichord), and having gone on from those to the more difficult and exciting dances in the French and English Suites, he can launch out on the perilous seas of the Forty-eight Preludes and Fugues (two in each key) and the Goldberg Variations, which, after taking the player through some of the most complicated and beautifully-coloured keyboard music in the world, end by giving him a couple of popular comic songs to play at the same time!

In the six Brandenburg Concertos there is the greatest fun and pleasure to be found by those who play flute, oboe, bassoon, horn, trumpet, piano, or any kind of stringed instrument. Violinists can play the concertos for solo violin and strings and the violin sonatas, or two of them can get together and play the beautiful 'double concerto.' Pianists also can tackle concertos for one, two, three, and even *four* keyboard instruments and orchestra!

If it were not for the organ music of Bach, an organist would be hard put to it to find sufficient good solo music to play. There are the early preludes and fugues to teach him how to play separate tunes with his two hands *and* his feet; there are the fantasias, toccatas, and fugues to enable him to 'show off' and to build vast and lofty domes of sound; and there are the chorale preludes, whose noble serenity can transport the listener to the very doors of heaven.

It has always been part of a church organist's duties to arrange special music for important days in the Church's year. Bach had this to do, and he actually wrote nearly 200 anthems, or *cantatas*, for his choir at St Thomas's. Leipzig. These cantatas were rather more elaborate than most of the anthems we hear in church now, and they were usually made up of choruses, solos, or duets, with a hymn at the end in which the congregation could sing with the choir. Bach also wrote some cantatas to celebrate occasions outside the church; the local nobleman might have a birthday, for instance, or a new rich landowner might settle in the district and be given 'musical honours' in the form of a humorous, affectionate cantata of welcome. Songs from these cantatas often crop up in your school singing, such as "Come, let us to the bagpipe's sound," "Sheep may safely graze," and "Spring comes laughing o'er the hill."

Bach's finest church music was written for Good Friday. On this day it was the custom of the Church in Germany to tell the story in music of our Lord's last days; His betrayal, arrest, trial, and crucifixion. The words of the story were of course taken from the Gospels, and were sung in a free manner by a narrator, usually called the 'Evangelist.' The chorus, like the 'extras' in a film, portrayed the 'crowd scenes'—lamenting, cursing, praying, deriding, following the tragic story throughout all its changing moods, and meditating with the soloists and the congregation on the various happenings. All the characters in the story—the High Priest, Pilate, Judas, St Peter, and Our Lord Himself—have their own parts to sing, and the whole effect is that of an opera, but without action or scenery. Bach's setting of the story as it is told in St Matthew's Gospel, known as the *St Matthew Passion*, is the most dramatic and powerful ever written; it is also so human and easily followed that no one who has heard it right through could possibly continue to call Bach's music "highbrow" and "mathematical." Here his music describes quite simply and plainly what is going on, as in the passage from Peter's 'Denial' scene, sung by the Evangelist, quoted on the opposite page.

There we hear the crowing of the cock, Peter's misery in the face of what he had done, and the sound of his weeping. It is *human* music, expressing the feelings of people —their moods of sorrow and joy, love and anger; and this applies to all the music of Bach for those who care to listen lovingly to it.

Bach also set to music the Passion story as told by St John; this and the Mass in B minor complete the list of his large choral works. The Mass is a setting of the Latin words used in the Roman Catholic Church for chorus, soloists, and orchestra. It is far too long and huge to be used as part of the church service, but to hear it or to sing in it 'just as music' is one of the most moving and exciting experiences in the whole of music. Again, it is music for the ordinary people, not merely for the clever musician.

In writing about Bach's music, I have used one or two words, such as *fugue, toccata, concerto,* and others, which may puzzle you. As several of these apply to Handel's music too I shall explain what they all mean at the end of this chapter, and at the same time give you some idea of how the music of these composers was performed.

It is obvious that Johann Sebastian Bach was a 'stay-at-home' musician. The happenings in the great outer world meant little to him; wars could be won and lost, kings

The *St Matthew Passion*, by J. S. Bach

and queens die and others be crowned, while Bach went about his business of composing, teaching, and playing, with nothing more exciting than an occasional row with the church authorities to bother him, and only a few trips to neighbouring towns to cause him to travel beyond the short path between his house and his church. He made his own world, and was content to live in it.

Bach was born in 1685, and in that year, in the same country, was born another musical baby whose future was to be vastly different. It was to be a story of constant travel, of having to be in favour with kings and queens as well as singers, players, and audiences in order to make a living, of musical plottings and the rough-and-tumble of politics, and even of a complete change of nationality—from German to English. This child was the son of a doctor; his name was George Frederick Handel. Now, if you were to approach any musical friend and ask him what first came into his head when you said the word "Handel" he would most certainly exclaim "Messiah!" So famous and beloved is Handel's *Messiah* that it seems to shine in our eyes like a great white light, blinding us to everything else he wrote. In it is contained everything that we love about Handel's music. There are the solos—"He shall feed His flock," "How beautiful are the feet," and "Comfort ye, my people!" beautiful and fine tunes which 'sing themselves,' and "But who may abide," "Why do the nations," and "Rejoice greatly," which demand of even the greatest singers all the skill and dramatic force they can give. And, of course, there are the choruses which, ranging from the vigorous and complicated "Amen" chorus to the great, massive "Hallelujah" chorus, have delighted and enthralled all choirs for two hundred years. Nowhere else in Handel's enormous output of music is there to be found such variety, and such deep feeling.

But Handel was fifty-six when he wrote *Messiah*, and had only seventeen more years to live. What had happened before *Messiah*? Along what thorny path did

Handel travel towards his position as the most famous Englishman of his time? At the outset, as a small boy, he had to contend with his father, who thought it was far too risky to try and make a living out of music. Soon, however, his talent began to be noticed by important people in the district—the local squire heard the young Handel playing the chapel organ; the organist himself offered to give him lessons on the spot; a member of the royal family had a word with Handel's father, and achieved a reluctant consent to the boy's studying music on condition that he worked hard at his general subjects at the Grammar School. At twelve he was assistant organist at the city church; at eighteen he had qualified in law at the University, because his father had wished him to. From that time onward it was to be music. Off he went to Hamburg to work at the opera-house, coaching the singers, playing the violin in the orchestra, playing accompaniments on the harpsichord, and doing any odd job about the place which would add to his training and experience as a practical musician. At the age of nineteen he wrote his first opera, and had the thrilling experience of seeing it produced on the stage. A year later he left for Italy.

In Florence, Rome, and Venice Handel found himself at the fountainhead of the popular music of the day. He heard it, learned how to write it, and proceeded to copy it. He was now all ready for his attack on London, where he arrived, at the age of twenty-five, to find all the audiences longing for the joyous, sparkling Italian music that was becoming so fashionable, but which there was no one to provide. He had, it is true, accepted a musical post in Germany, that of Court Musician to the Elector George Louis of Hanover, but what could that have mattered to a young adventurer like Handel, when London was so obviously waiting for his music? One might as well expect a brilliant young fast bowler to stay with his village team when the county was wanting him.

Handel's first London task was to write an opera, *Rinaldo*, which he finished in fourteen days, and which was produced in fine style at the Queen's Theatre, in the Haymarket. It seems from the newspaper reports of the time that this first effort of Handel's in London was the most striking and successful event of the season. He could not have made a better start.

He did go back to Hanover afterwards, however, but we soon find him applying for leave to come to London again, and this time he overstayed his leave. He was not to know then that the captain of his village team was to become captain of the M.C.C.—that George Louis, Elector of Hanover, was destined to become George I of England in 1714. The meeting in England must have been an uncomfortable one for both of them. It has been said that Handel appeased the King by composing the *Water Music*, to be played on a barge as the King made a river-journey on the Thames. Whether or not this story is true, it is a pleasant one. Whatever happened, Handel was speedily forgiven, and became as popular at the royal court as he was with the audiences who came to hear his operas.

And so Handel came to London, to be the greatest and most popular musician of his day. One of his strongest talents (which only failed him once) was that of knowing what the public wanted, and giving it to them in full measure. Audiences wanted sparkling, empty Italian operas; Handel produced over forty of them. Later, when men's thoughts in England had taken a more serious turn, he gave them operatic works based on serious subjects, in which the performers sang without acting, as on the concert platform. These were called *oratorios*. Only between his Italian operas and his oratorios did Handel lose sight of his audiences' wishes. For some reason he was slow in noticing that the English people were tiring of Italian opera, that they were wanting their music based on the really English songs they knew so well, and that there was already such an opera, called *The Beggar's Opera*, running in London at that time, and drawing packed audiences in the same way that an American musical

comedy draws them to-day. No showman can afford such
a mistake, not even Handel, and for him it meant several
years of poverty and illness until, in his middle forties, he
began to write his oratorios. Though this sort of entertainment was slow to attract audiences at first—even
Messiah fell flat when it was first heard in London—the
oratorios did keep Handel going financially until the end
of his days.

The life-story of George Frederick Handel, musician,
adventurer, showman, could go on for the rest of this
book. It is a story of violent happenings—huge, fashionable successes in the theatre; fights among the audiences
between those who liked him and those who were madly
jealous of him; furious scenes with rival singers, in one of
which Handel suspended a particularly angry soprano
out of an upstairs window, threatening to let go of her if
she did not begin to behave herself that instant; great
acts of generosity when he was able to afford them:
severe illnesses which attacked him just as his fortunes
were at their lowest; total blindness due to a clumsy
operation on his eyes; periods of composing when he
seemed to be caught up in a white-hot flame of inspiration, as during his writing of *Messiah* (which he completed in twenty-three days), when he said, "I think I did
see all heaven before me, and the great God Himself."

As with Bach, however, Handel's life is only important
if it can give us a clearer understanding of his music.
This was a life of effort to give the musical public what
they wanted, and to keep in favour with royalty, who set
the musical fashions of the day.

The noble English audiences, who had lots of leisure
time, loved to pass an evening listening to opera in the
Italian style, which had to be attractive enough to keep
them awake; that is to say, there must be plenty of good
tunes to show off the singers. All the things we need in
opera nowadays—dramatic situations, a good story, the
characters expressed in music which fits them—were
much less important than a handful of songs with simple

tunes and plenty of room for trills and runs. Handel provides these in abundance in his operas, and if there is any fault to find with them it is that they were too good for both the operas and the audiences. How enjoyable it is to sing this line from the opera *Semele*:

Where e'er you walk,, cool gales shall fan the glade.

And how well-loved is this song from *Xerxes*, sung by a beery old king to the foliage of a tree under which he is having a shady nap in the middle of the day:

Yes, the famous 'Handel's Largo' started life in an opera, and when you hear it played on solemn occasions it is convenient to forget about the dissolute old monarch. The tune will live as long as there are people to sing it and play it.

Living very much in the world, a naturalized Englishman, and very dependent on royal favour, Handel was never slow to bring out music to celebrate English historical events. There were four Coronation Anthems for George II, funeral marches on the death of famous people, choruses of praise for British victories on the battlefield. Handel was indeed the official minstrel of England's fortunes, and it is not surprising that on his death he joined the company of the great in the vaults of Westminster Abbey.

It is his oratorios, however, which seem to keep the firmest hold on musicians these days. *Messiah*, *Israel in Egypt*, and *Judas Maccabæus* have been sung for two hundred years by choruses containing people who can read music and sing, and people who cannot; scholars

THE HOUSE IN BONN WHERE BEETHOVEN WAS BORN
Beethoven lived here until he was seventeen.
By courtesy of the B.B.C.

AN ORATORIO PERFORMANCE

In front of the conductor are the soloists (from left to right:
soprano, contralto, tenor, and bass). Behind them is the orchestra,
and then the chorus.

"Picture Post" Library

A SCENE FROM ONE OF WAGNER'S OPERAS

This photograph was taken during a performance at the
Royal Opera House, Covent Garden.

Photo Wilfrid Newton

and peasants; townsmen and countrymen. Handel's music is performed by the cleverest musicians in the world because it is great music; it is enjoyed by ordinary people because it is simple. He is a great painter who can produce fine pictures by using no more than three primary colours. Handel, using only three musical sounds, or sometimes only two, could build huge cathedrals of glorious sound, so that we, when we wander into them, can say with him, "I think I did see all Heaven before me. . . ."

King of Kings and Lord of Lords

Messiah, by G. F. Handel

When he thinks of a line of the Bible which strikes home to us by its very simplicity, such as "I know that my Redeemer liveth," he sets it to music in the simplest and most direct way:

I know that my Re – deem – er liv – eth.

Messiah, by G. F. Handel

The soprano voice, singing the first two words with no accompaniment, seems to be saying, "It's not a question of 'I think,' or 'I hope,' or 'I've been told,' but—'I know!'"

Messiah was written in twenty-three days, and takes just over three hours to perform. It is obvious that Handel must have used a sort of convenient shorthand to get it all down. This shorthand, used by all the eighteenth-century composers, was called *figured bass,* or *continuo,* and it worked as follows:

Most tunes in the world need at least two things: a melody, and a *bass* to support it. These two things make the skeleton of the music, which must then be filled out with flesh. The flesh of music is the *harmony*—the sounds which fill in the gap between the melody and the bass, giving the skeleton the rounded, rich appearance of the complete person. This harmony need not be written out by the composer; he can show it by using a 'code' of figures, which he writes under the bass-line. So all he need write is the melody, the bass, and the figures underneath the bass.

When the song is performed the harmonies are filled in by the man at the keyboard (the organ or the harpsichord), who in those days was trained to read the figures just as a stenographer can read the squiggles of her shorthand. Here is an example, the melody, the bass, and the figures (written down by the composer) are shown in large type, and the harmonies (made up by the keyboard-player from the figures) are shown in small type:

Messiah, by G. F. Handel

In that way it was possible to write down long tunes in a very short time, though the playing of them depended a great deal on the skill of the continuo-player, as the man at the keyboard was called.

Handel did not altogether neglect instrumental players, though we seem to have been thinking about nothing but his vocal music so far. There are twelve Grand Concertos for string-players to enjoy, twelve concertos for organ and strings, which are light-hearted works to be played during the intervals of his oratorios, and some sixteen suites for harpsichord players (pianists nowadays), which Handel wrote for the two daughters of George II. All these are not so enjoyable as Bach's instrumental music, but they are worth exploring for the moments of real beauty and excitement dotted about them.

We compared Bach fancifully to the sea. Handel's music is, perhaps, a mountain torrent, rushing headlong from the heights, digging deep channels in the hard cliff-face of musical history. Many of these channels have dried up; very few musicians these days have ever seen a performance of one of his many operas; it is very rarely that his orchestral music finds its way into concert programmes. Only a handful of his oratorios are with us year after year, and these give abiding joy; the torrent has spent itself.

Handel's countryman, Johann Sebastian Bach, still remains; not 'brook,' but the sea itself, the supreme master of the art and the craft of music.

SOME DEFINITIONS

Toccata

A rapid keyboard-piece, often in free time (*i.e.*, without any orderly, regular pulse running through it), designed to show off the skill of the player.

Fugue

A form of composition which depends on the interweaving of parts, as did the polyphonic music of Palestrina, though it is more often played than sung. One part enters with a scrap of tune and is joined by several others in turn, obeying strict rules. It is like a discussion which ranges round a subject, departs from it occasionally, becomes heated now and then, and ends in complete agreement.

Passacaglia

A piece of music in which a short phrase (only a few bars) is repeated over and over again; as soon as it gets to the end it starts again. This is not the tune, however; it is most often in the bass, and acts as a sort of scaffolding for the piece, which, like a stately building, grows round it. The word comes from Spain, and means something like 'walking down the street!'

Cantata and Sonata

At this time in history they meant 'a piece to be sung' and 'a piece to be played.' A cantata is a miniature oratorio, with choruses and solos, joined with recitative (though it can be for just one voice, with accompaniment). A sonata is also a work in several sections, and is usually played on one or two instruments. Cantatas have not changed much since Bach's time, but sonatas continued to grow in importance, as we shall see later.

Suite

A favourite name for groups of instrumental pieces in Bach's time. They were usually for keyboard, and consisted of popular dances of the time (gavottes, minuets, sarabands, bourrées), but Bach wrote several suites for orchestra. The term is still often used—as in Tchaikovsky's *Nut-cracker Suite*.

Concerto

A form of music in which a player, or a group of players, is given a 'star' part, with the rest of the orchestra accompanying. Bach and Handel wrote for groups of players as a rule, but after their time it was usual to have one soloist only, who, like the chief player in a Shakespeare play, held the stage.

SIGNPOST TWO

The Development of Sonata Form and the Reform of Opera

IMAGINE that you are sitting in the audience at an orchestral concert. You have just heard a suite or a concerto by J. S. Bach, and you are now settling down to listen to a symphony by Haydn. The symphony would not have been playing more than five minutes or so before you noticed an enormous difference in the sound that was reaching you. Even if you had not had a great deal of practice in listening to music you would feel as if you had suddenly stepped from one room into another, with different furnishings, a different shape, and different views from the windows. Yet Bach was still alive, and still writing music, when Haydn was already seventeen. How and why had the sound of music changed so suddenly?

To begin with, the change was not sudden, though it was certainly rapid. J. S. Bach lived a quiet, sheltered life in Leipzig, away from the busy, throbbing world of artistic progress, and even during his lifetime his music was becoming old-fashioned in the eyes of the younger musicians. Even his own sons—Friedemann, Johann Christian, and the brilliant Carl Philipp Emanuel, all important composers—were heard to pour a certain amount of scorn on their father's method of writing music in counterpoint (weaving and contrasting tunes and rhythms). They and their young fellow-musicians throughout Europe were thinking their music out on different lines.

Very broadly speaking, the changes taking place were to be found

1. In the actual sounds of the orchestra;
2. In the 'pattern' on which the music was written;
3. In the path along which the composers' minds moved when they were planning their music.

In Chapter 2 ('Ways of making Music') we saw how the orchestra gradually became more settled in design, passing from the haphazard collection of instruments of Monteverde's time to the more orderly plan of strings and wind which Bach and Handel controlled from the keyboard of the harpsichord, and then to the sensitive, colourful groupings of woodwind, brass, percussion, and strings used by Haydn and Mozart, who dispensed with the keyboard and conducted by gesture. It was by the efforts and experiments of Bach's sons, of Rameau in France, and of such minor composers as Carl Stamitz of Mannheim (where there was an excellent orchestra to experiment with) that the 'Haydn and Mozart' orchestra settled down into the form in which we know it now. They made a lot of mistakes; their groups of wind instruments were often far too powerful for the strings, and were too often used just to come in with loud blasts in loud parts of the music. But gradually by trial and error, they groped their way towards the ideal of orchestral sound; the use of instruments to give the greatest possible variety of *tone-colour* to the music.

Just as a beautiful building is far more than a mere cluster of rooms and hutments, so is fine music far more than a collection of tunes. Any beautiful work of art must have shape and design, and music is no exception. Far from flowing on and on like water from a tap, it has always fallen into firm, clear patterns, and at this time a new, great pattern was emerging which has formed the basis of all large musical works from 1750 to the present day. This pattern, or 'form,' is called *sonata form*. Why is 'sonata form' a new pattern, and how did it differ from the old patterns? When J. S. Bach sat down to write an orchestral work we might imagine him saying, "Here I am, about to start on a long journey. Like a high-powered railway-engine, I must push on for all I'm worth so that I arrive at my destination on time. The train which I am pulling has all sorts of different passengers aboard (various musical tunes and rhythms). We will pass through valleys, plains, forests, mountains; some passengers will like it all, others will be bored. But, whatever happens, we will all arrive at the end of the line in good spirits and quite happy about it all." Bach takes us from Point A to Point B along a route full of interest, and we follow him enthusiastically because we know where he is going, and that he will arrive on time. Listen to the third Brandenburg Concerto and you will see just what this means. From the beginning to the end of the first movement the music is kept in motion by a single rhythmic 'tick,' which, like the easy stride of a cross-country runner, is never allowed to falter. That one musical idea drives the music on to its destination.

Now Haydn or Mozart, about to write the first movement of a symphony, would address us in a different manner. They would say, "Attention please! I've got two important ideas to put before you. Here they are. Have you got them? Now this is what I think about them. The first idea needs breaking up a bit, so that we can examine it point by point; the second we can perhaps enlarge upon, put it more strongly and clearly. Yes, I think we have dealt with them as thoroughly as we can, so let's put the bits together again and sum up." The two musical ideas which are to be subjects for discussion are usually contrasted in mood—the first is often stern and commanding, like a parade-ground order, and the second more tuneful and sympathetic. They are called officially the *first subject* and the *second subject*. The first part of the movement, in which these two subjects are stated, or expounded, is called the *exposition*; the following part, where the ideas are broken up, discussed, and developed, is called the *development*; and the final section, the summing-up and the restating of the two ideas, is called the *recapitulation*.

Why did these 'new' composers after the death of Bach begin to adopt this pattern instead of the 'journey from A to B' pattern which had stood them in such good stead? The answer is perhaps to be found in the first Signpost chapter, when we considered the first signs of a break-away from church music, and the first attempts to link music up with drama, in opera and oratorio. Whether they were writing operas or not, the later musicians found their minds turning on the possibilities of *contrast* in all music—the stern, strong hero (first subject) and the gentle heroine (second subject); the closer interlinking of their lives and emotions, and their disagreements (development); and their living happily ever after (recapitulation). In nearly all plays we find that Act 1 introduces our hero and heroine and starts the story; Act 2 contains all the trials and difficulties—the things that go wrong, the closer knowledge of the main characters; Act 3 sees them safely through it all, and safely reconciled.

The composer who did most to work out this new pattern was Bach's son, Carl Philipp Emanuel (usually known as C. P. E. Bach). In C. P. E. Bach's music there is an amusing mixture of the old and the new styles. For instance, he will sometimes introduce his first and second subjects in perfectly correct manner, and then he will develop them in his father's finest 'cross-country run' style, for all the world as if the great old man were looking over his shoulder and saying, "My son, write your music as *I* taught you!" Neither father nor son could have known, however, that C. P. E. Bach was working out a musical design which was to be followed by every great composer from that day to this.

It is difficult to avoid talking about rivers and streams when one is discussing the history of music. For the fact remains that music was approaching another period, as it had done in the days of Palestrina and, later, in those of

J. S. Bach. The new pattern, sonata form, was fixing itself in the minds of composers, and was to lead to the great symphonies, sonatas, and concertos of Haydn, Mozart, and Beethoven. Flowing to meet this stream was another one, that of opera.

In the last Signpost chapter we left opera in the grip of conceited singers who had dragged it down into the realms of utter stupidity and nonsense. But already, in Paris, something was being done by Lully to restore it to the wonderful level at which the Italian composer Monteverde had left it. Now, in the middle years of the eighteenth century, an Austrian composer was coming to the fore who was shortly to carry out an operatic revolution. His name was Christoph Willibald von Gluck. Weary to death of the fashionable operas he had been writing, in which nothing mattered but the singers, he decided, come what may, to risk presenting his audiences in Vienna with an opera which would embody his ideas of what opera ought to be. He accordingly set himself some rules, which can be put down like this:

1. An opera is a dramatic story, and the story must come first. It must not be brought to a complete standstill while some vain, stupid singer shrieks and caterwauls nonsensical songs which have nothing whatever to do with the plot.

2. The whole point of an opera is that the characters in the story, the situations they find themselves in, and their own joys and sorrows, are made more powerful and impressive by the music they sing and the sounds of the orchestra. Therefore there must not be a single song, chorus, duet, trio, quartet, or orchestral effect which does not fit in with the characters or the story.

3. All songs, choruses, orchestral pieces, and the rest, must follow each other in proper order, just like the events of the story upon which the opera is based.

4. The overture must prepare the audience for the mood and the drama of the opera.

Gluck chose for his first opera the well-worn story of Orpheus and Eurydice. Orpheus, heartbroken by the death of his lovely wife Eurydice, wanders down into the underworld to seek her. At the gates he meets the Furies, and Cerberus, the many-headed dog, whose task it is to keep mortals out. As he sings to them, however, they relent, and he passes in to find his wife. His singing is of such beauty that he is given permission to take her back to earth with him if he promises not to look back at her on their journey. Of course, he cannot resist the temptation, and she is lost to him again.

Now, it is obvious that a story like this, built around a famous singer, Orpheus, will give a great many opportunities for songs, especially in the scene where Orpheus is trying to sing his way past the guardians of the underworld. In the bad old days the entire story would have been held up here while Orpheus sang one song after another, whether they were part of the opera or not. Gluck, however, gives Orpheus three songs, separated from each other by the chorus of Furies, whose shouts become more and more subdued as Orpheus charms them. The first of these songs is only forty-three bars long, and lasts about two minutes, the second is twenty-three bars long, and the third fifteen. But the whole scene, so short and to the point, is perfect opera. The pleadings of Orpheus become shorter and more intense, while the mutterings of the Furies become longer and more peaceful. The story goes on, with every note of the music fitting into it; like the lighting and the scenery, the vocal and orchestral sounds help to bring characters and plot to life. The longest and most tragic song is just where we would expect it to be—at the moment when Orpheus looks back to Eurydice and loses her for ever. The very tune itself passes through the emotions which Orpheus endured—heartbreaking grief, fierce remorse, resignation.

Gluck's new type of opera finally won the day, but not without a strenuous struggle. Audiences were indignant and bewildered. It was just as if the local variety theatre, which people had been attending week after week to see the latest comedian, suddenly announced that henceforward there would be nothing but Shakespeare plays. Undaunted, Gluck went on producing his stern, classical operas, and began to consider seeking a more appreciative audience in another important centre of opera—Paris. Here Jean Philippe Rameau (whose operas had influenced Gluck) had been trying to stem the flow of nonsensical Italian opera into the capital, but after his death in 1764 the Parisian opera-goers were again at the mercy of visiting Italian opera companies.

Largely owing to the influence of Marie Antoinette (who had been Gluck's pupil) Gluck was able to produce an opera, *Iphigenia in Aulis*, in Paris in 1774. Two years later (when, after several further productions, Gluck was at the height of his reputation in Paris) an Italian opera composer called Nicola Piccinni, who was very famous at that time, was invited to come to the capital and produce a new opera there. Those who disliked Gluck's reforms set up Piccinni as his rival, and for some years a 'war' raged between the partisans of the two composers. The contest was fast and furious, and tempers ran high; the pure, serene, classical work of Gluck was pitted against the frivolous, lightsome nonsense of Piccinni. Gluck presented two more operas, driving home his new ideas, and won the day. Dramatic opera had come to stay, and was soon to be taken up in accordance with Gluck's ideas by Mozart, Beethoven, Weber, and even the Italians themselves.

C. P. E. Bach's new musical pattern and Gluck's new plan for opera, the wide scope of sonata form and the rich emotions conjured up in the new operatic music were the two important streams of thought flowing into the second half of the 1700's.

Joseph Haydn was born in 1732, and Wolfgang Amadeus Mozart in 1756.

6

Haydn and Mozart

FOR a time now the beam of your historical spotlight has been rather out of focus; it has been a diffused light, gently illuminating Bach in Leipzig, Handel in London, C. P. E. Bach in Berlin, Rameau in Paris, and Gluck in the Austrian capital, Vienna. From J. S. Bach, the great climax of the old polyphonic period, to his clever and adventurous son, C. P. E. Bach, and Gluck, the forward-looking opera composer, there stretches a short but very exciting time of change and exploration. So short was it that, looking back on the 1700's, it seems that the face of music changed overnight. So let us pick out one particular year at random—any one will do—say, 1781. In that year a forty-nine-year-old musician called Joseph Haydn, who had come from the Hungarian border many years ago to Vienna as a choirboy, met a brilliant young composer aged twenty-five, who was in Vienna after being discharged from the service of the Archbishop of Salzburg. This was Wolfgang Amadeus Mozart, to whose father Haydn said, "I declare to you on my honour that I consider your son the greatest composer I have ever heard." In this same year an eleven-year-old boy was growing up in a little house in Bonn, who six years later was to find his way to Vienna to have a few lessons in music from Mozart, and then from Haydn. His name was Ludwig van Beethoven. Years later there could be seen in a little coffee-house in Vienna (it is still there) the middle-aged Beethoven sitting sunk in thought at one table, while at a near-by one sat a plump young man gazing timidly at him, too shy ever to speak. He was a schoolmaster's son called Franz Schubert.

Haydn, Mozart, Beethoven, Schubert—Vienna; there can be no doubt as to which part of Europe our spotlight is to rest upon. All had finished their life's work—and their lives too—by 1830, but they caused Vienna to take its place with London and Rome as the third great focal-point of music's splendour.

Joseph Haydn went to the Choir School of St Stephen's, Vienna, when he was eight years old. There he learnt to play the harpsichord and the violin, and was given a smattering of general knowledge. His beautiful treble voice was often heard and admired both in St Stephen's and in the Imperial Chapel, and his mischievous behaviour was the despair of his teachers. Even the Empress herself once had to send one of her servants to tell that "blond blockhead" to come down from the scaffolding surrounding a new part of the Palace, and it was his cutting off of a fellow-pupil's pigtail (in the course of trying out a new pair of scissors) which caused him to be finally expelled. Before that, however, his voice was beginning to change, and when the Empress remarked to her Director of Music that young Haydn was "crowing like a cock" it was obvious that he would have to leave soon. The Choir School did nothing to help him, and Haydn, now about eighteen, had to work out his own life. He borrowed some money and a "worm-eaten old harpsi-chord" from kindly friends, and set up house in an attic. His hours of scribbling music at St Stephen's had con-vinced him that he must be a composer, and now, without delay, he set out to learn his job.

His teacher was Carl Philipp Emanuel Bach—not the man himself, but the music he had written: the keyboard sonatas and the symphonies which showed the workings of the new pattern, sonata form. For some sixteen hours a day Haydn worked at this music, finding out how it was put together and soaking himself in the sound of it.

C. P. E. Bach, then in his thirties, was already a cele-brated popular composer; he was not to know that his greatest achievement was to be the worthy forerunner of

Joseph Haydn, or that, years later, Mozart would say of him, "He is the father, and we are all the children."

It was not long before local musicians began to hear about Haydn, this pleasant, studious young man from the country, who was already trying his hand at some interesting church music. Soon he was a welcome guest at houses where amateur singers and players gathered to make music. When he was twenty-three he was invited to join a musical party at a large country house. The guests were to stay for some weeks, playing and studying as much music as they could lay their hands on. No one could have realized how important this visit was to be for the future of music. In the house was the usual group of players to be found in most large, cultured houses— some wind instruments and a few good strings. Haydn, with his head buzzing with C. P. E. Bach's musical experiments, quietly proceeded to write several pieces of music for these players to play. These included works for strings and wind together, and others for the four best string-players: two violinists, a viola-player, and a cellist. They were in several sections—often five, but the number later settled down to four. And so, quite accidentally and without any sensation, there came into being the first symphony and the first string quartet in the form in which we know them now.

What does this mean? How did Haydn alter the ideas of previous composers? Broadly speaking, he found he had made two changes: (a) in the *shape* of a long piece of music, and (b) in the *balance* of the instruments which were to play it. Previously, when composers wished to write a long piece of music (that is to say, a piece of music in several sections, or *movements*) they tended to use the following patterns:

1. Variations on a tune.
2. A set of dances—gavottes, minuets, sarabands, jigs, etc.—separated by 'airs' (just tunes) to give added variety (known as a *suite*).

3. The simple pattern, 'slow (played twice)—quick—slow' (known as the 'French Overture').

4. An equally simple pattern, 'Quick—slow—quick' (known as the 'Italian Overture').

5. A *rondo* (in which the main tune keeps coming round, like the refrain of a song.

Haydn's hero, C. P. E. Bach, preferred the 'Italian' pattern; thus many of Haydn's earlier works followed it. Haydn, like the true countryman he was, loved folk-tunes and dances, and it was not long before we find him slipping into his symphonies the most popular dance of the day, the minuet. This came just after the slow movement; Haydn obviously felt that his audiences needed to listen to something lively and fairly short at that point. So gradually the pattern of a long piece of music was fixed by Haydn, who was continually experimenting and improving, and it is still in the front of a composer's mind when he begins to write a symphony or a string quartet. It can be expressed like this:

First Movement. In 'sonata form.' Quick and clever, needing quite a lot of attention on the listener's part. Sometimes with a slow introduction.

Second Movement. Slow and very melodious.

Third Movement. A minuet. Usually brisk and heavy, as if the dancers were dancing in hob-nailed boots!

Finale. A *rondo*. Quick, and easier to follow than the first movement because the main tune recurs.

We know from the last Signpost chapter that composers had been experimenting with the *balance* of sounds when they were writing for the orchestra. They were exploring means of combining wind instruments with strings so that the music would be all the richer for the differences in colour between the various instruments.

Thanks to the way his life worked out, Haydn was able to push forward this experimenting and exploration to a triumphant conclusion, for the time being at least. In 1761 he was appointed as a full-time Director of Music to

Prince Nicholas Esterhazy in his establishment at Eisen-stadt. There, at Esterhazy's palace, he stayed for thirty years, comfortably housed and with a regular salary—-and with an orchestra of excellent players to play his music. Every new effect, every blending and contrasting of wood-wind with strings, of solo instrument with full orchestra, of adventurous harmony, could be tried out and judged immediately. He also had two theatres and a chapel, complete with picked singers. Perhaps no composer has ever had such an excellent opportunity to carry out his musical plans and bring his visions to life, especially as his employer, recognizing that Haydn was a genius, gave him a completely free hand. So he turned out symphonies to be listened to on special occasions, *divertimenti* ('amusement-pieces') to aid digestion after supper, and church music and keyboard pieces to his heart's content. The one sad element in the life of this happy, kindly man seemed to be his wife, who had no interest in his music, and whom he could not stand at any price!

Haydn's love of practical jokes, so troublesome during his schooldays, stayed with him all his life, and some-times got into his music. In one symphony (the 'Surprise') he causes the orchestra to make a loud bang right in the middle of the slow movement tune, just to make sure that the audience is not dropping off to sleep after a good supper; in another (the 'Farewell') he arranges that the orchestral players come to the end of their music one by one, and, putting out the candles on their music-stands, steal away from the scene. This was a gentle reminder to the Prince that the musicians were overdue for their holiday. His lovely oratorio, *The Creation*, is full of pic-torial noises; the weather (rain, hail, snow, thunder, and lightning) and the animals (lions, tigers, stags, horses, cows, sheep, insects) all have their little orchestral pic-tures—even the worm, creeping "in long dimension, with sinuous trace," is honoured with an appropriate piece of slithery music.

Although Haydn lived in a palace and was the friend

of princes he remained a simple countryman. Even when he was a small boy his intensely musical ear must have picked up all the boisterous songs and dances which he would constantly hear at village festivities; near the Ester-hazy palace there was a well-known village inn where, we know, he used to sit during his free evenings, listening to the singing of the local peasants. All his music is soaked with this healthy influence; it gives to the quartets and symphonies the pleasant tang of a peat fire or the glow of matured red sandstone. In one of the biggest and finest of his symphonies, the 'London' (No. 104 in D), we hear a minuet which would never be danced in a palace ball-room; it is for the barn or the village square, to be trodden out with hobnailed boots. Later, in the same symphony, there is a very countrified tune, played as if to the drone of a bagpipe:

There must be very few school orchestras who have not tried to play movements from Haydn's symphonies, and every amateur quartet has rejoiced in the quartets, which range from the simplicity of the early ones (with the very elementary cello parts) to the rich, colourful weaving of string sound of the 'Emperor' quartet (where we hear the hymn-tune "Praise the Lord, ye heavens adore Him"). Pianists can join in the trios for violin, cello, and piano, in which the cellist usually has an easy time (but the pianist has to work hard, as you will find when you try the G major 'Gipsy Rondo' trio!). The pianist can also play the sonatas, each of which is a voyage of exploration; in these Haydn seems to have put down all his random ideas, just as if he were keeping a diary—one rarely knows what is going to happen on the next page. Every choral society must have revelled in singing *The Creation* and *The Seasons;* and only recently choirs have discovered the magnificent Mass in D minor, known as the 'Nelson Mass.' Haydn was writing this at the time of the battle of Aboukir, and it is reported that it was performed during a visit of Lord Nelson to Eisenstadt in 1800, and that Nelson traded his watch for the pen with which it was written. When Vaughan Williams first heard this work he described it as "the most thrilling musical experience of my old age."

Soloists other than pianists have not been well served by Haydn. Of concertos there are one or two for piano (the D major is a good one to do in school concerts), and of course there is the delightful Trumpet Concerto. A concerto for cello has been known and loved for years as the work of Haydn, but it is more than likely that it was written by one of his pupils; there are also some concertos for violin, flute, horn, double-bass, and oboe which have not yet found their way very often into concert programmes.

Singers, too, have not got a great deal of choice in Haydn's music; there are some songs (called 'canzonets') of which only *My Mother bids me bind my Hair* and *The Mermaid* are likely to be heard in programmes; there are no operas which can be produced on the modern stage.

It was in the way he made instrumental music grow, through his symphonies and chamber music, that Joseph Haydn helped music along its historical path. In the course of making lots of mistakes—trying out new ways of writing music, and discarding many of them—he breathed into music a breath of fresh life which was to have its effect for nearly half a century. As 'Papa Haydn' he must have been a genial, kindly man; during the bombardment of Vienna by the French in the last year of his life he was found reassuring his servants that nothing would happen to them while he was there to take care of them, and after Vienna had fallen he was very moved to receive a visit from a French officer, who sang to him "In native worth" from *The Creation*.

When Haydn first met Wolfgang Amadeus Mozart in 1781 the two became lifelong friends. Everything about their lives was different. Mozart was one of those extraordinary people who seem to be born with all the knowledge and skill they need for their work; he never *learned* anything—he just *remembered*. Even at the age of four he was composing little pieces in the 'new' style. His father Leopold, himself a famous violin-teacher, soon realized that there was a musical genius in the family, and took the boy and his sister Marianne (who also showed musical talent) on a tour round Europe as petted child wonders. It says a lot for young Wolfgang's strength of character that he was able to survive this unsettled existence and early popularity.

At six he played at the Emperor's court in Vienna, where he saw how his future public, the nobility, lived and thought; the next year he was taken to Paris, where he left a handful of violin sonatas with the young Princess. Next came London, where George III doted on him, and where the eight-year-old boy heard his first Italian opera.

Now the strain of constant travelling and playing was beginning to show itself in spells of illness, and Leopold wisely took the little boy and his sister home to Salzburg, where he resumed Wolfgang's musical instruction.

At fourteen Mozart went to Italy with his father to learn more about the Italian style of opera, which had attracted him in London, and which he had already tried his hand at in Salzburg. During a visit to the Sistine Chapel in Rome he astonished the authorities by memorizing a piece of choral music after one hearing, and writing it down with hardly a mistake.

By this time Mozart had as a background to all this travelling and composing a post on the musical staff of the Archbishop of Saltzburg. This was the only settled post he was ever to have, and it was far too irksome to last for long. The Archbishop was the worst type of employer for an artist; he resented Mozart's growing fame, refused to allow him leave of absence to give concerts in other towns, paid him badly, overworked him, and made him live in the servants' quarters. Mozart spent some years in his service, but the ill-treatment was more than he could stand, and at the age of twenty-five he left the post—but not before he had been literally kicked out of the Archbishop's house by the High Steward, after a bitter scene.

This unhappy ending to Mozart's only settled job is important. It meant that Mozart, from that time, had to make a living by writing and performing music, just as a confectioner does by selling sweets. He was the first *professional composer*—that is to say, the first composer who did not have behind him a church appointment, a wealthy patron, or a directorship of an opera house to bring in a steady income, and his years of strife with the Archbishop really marked the end (in music) of the patronage system, which meant the employing of musicians by rich noblemen to organize the music in their private houses. Never again was a great composer comfortably settled in a congenial job as Haydn was at the Esterhazy Palace—and never again was a musical genius obliged to put up with such behaviour as the Archbishop's towards Mozart.

Now Mozart—playing, teaching, and composing—was at the mercy of the public, and he had ten more years to live. These years were a story of wavering fortunes, hard work, and travelling. He wrote, "The whole morning, till two o'clock, is taken up with lesson-giving, then we dine. After dinner I am obliged to give my poor stomach a short hour for digestion; it is only in the evening that I can write anything, and this not always, on account of my frequently being invited to concerts." And yet the symphonies (forty-one of them), the piano concertos (twenty-three), the string quartets, trios, and sonatas were somehow written; there were also the operas.

Idomeneo in Munich, *Il Seraglio* and *The Marriage of Figaro* in Vienna, *Don Giovanni* in Prague (where Mozart was greeted with a flourish of trumpets when he came in to conduct)—it was opera which buzzed in Mozart's mind for most of his short life. In his symphonies the contrasting tunes are so often the Hero and the Heroine; in the piano music the low notes in the left hand and the high tunes in the right hand are surely Suzanna and the Count in *Figaro*, having one of their mischievous discussions; the slow movements become operatic arias, decorated and shaped to show off the *voices* rather than the *instrument* they are written for. If a pianist, or a violinist, or an orchestra cannot get a Mozart tune absolutely right they just need to be reminded to "make it *sing*, as if you were an operatic singer."

All great composers *are* great because they give a special 'flavour' of their own to musical sound. J. S. Bach gave its a kind of spiritual sanity; Handel contributed huge effects built out of the simplest material; Haydn left with us a radiant healthiness. To Mozart we owe all that is exquisite and gracious in music. But there is nothing fragile or 'pretty' about his music; its grace is that of finely-tempered steel. In the rise and fall of his beautifully shaped tunes is a wealth of deep feelings, and in his harmonies there are shadows as well as warmth and light.

Unlike Haydn, Mozart did not take much notice of rustic folk-tunes; the minuets in his symphonies belong to the ballroom, not to the village green—but they are so full of feeling that they would make the dancers stop and listen. Though he liked to compose his music in the open air, he did not know much more about the sights and sounds of the countryside than what he could see and hear from the coach window during his incessant journeys.

Very happily married to a wife who was not at all a good housekeeper, Mozart had a struggle to make ends meet during the last years of his pathetically short life, but, until illness settled upon him, he showed in his music an ever wider and deeper feeling for the joys and sadnesses of human beings.

The last year of his life (1791) was the busiest. It began by his being asked to write the music for a fairy story to be acted in the courtyard of an inn. Mozart was half way through it when two things happened. First, he realized more and more that this 'fairy tale' was growing into a kind of fable with a moral; it was becoming far more serious and profound as it went on. (Finally, as *The Magic Flute*, it contained Mozart's deepest thoughts on the living of the good life, and was also an expression of his love of Freemasonry, which had occupied him for many years.) Secondly, a stranger arrived one day to commission Mozart to write a requiem (a Mass for the dead), for which he was to be paid a welcome sum of money. Mozart agreed to this, as he had not written any church music for many years; he was beset, however, by thoughts that the Requiem was really a sign of his approaching death. No sooner had he begun work on it than he was urgently asked to write an opera for a coronation in Prague. Ailing and haunted by the idea of death, he completed both operas, *The Magic Flute* and *La Clemenza di Tito*, and conducted their first performances.

Although by now very ill, he had already composed a good deal of the Requiem; but the effort proved too much for him. On December 4 the score was brought to him where he lay in bed at his home in Vienna; he realized, however, that he would be unable to finish it, and in the evening handed it over to his pupil Süssmayer, who completed it after his death. He died in the early hours of the next morning. His funeral was of the poorest; some of his close friends were driven back by a fierce storm before they had accompanied the hearse to the graveyard, and Mozart was buried alone, in a common grave, as paupers were.

None of Mozart's music is easy to perform by anyone

who is not a fine singer or player. His piano music was written to be played by himself—and he was the finest player of his day; his operatic songs make such demands on the breath, the intelligence, and the compass of the voice that only highly trained singers can manage them successfully. Orchestras of amateur players find that his symphonies and concertos show up their slightest mistake —they are written so clearly and require such perfection of playing. And yet so exquisitely simple and gracious do his melodies sound when they are sung and played by a great artist that one does not think of the control that is needed to make them sound like that. For every one in the musical world the name 'Mozart' will always stand for elegance, grace, and magical sound.

7

Beethoven and Schubert

FEW travellers pass through the West German town of Bonn without calling at a little house in a sloping street leading down from the market-place. Whether they are musicians or not they make a point of visiting the birthplace of a composer whose name every one knows as well as his own—Beethoven. They look in at the tiny attic bedroom where, in 1770, he was born; they stand on the tiny wedge-shaped patch of grass in the back garden where he must have learnt to walk and run; they examine the priceless set of stringed instruments hanging on the wall, which are taken down once a year and used by great players to perform his string quartets; and they are moved nearly to tears by the sight of his piano—mauled, battered, and wrecked in the composer's frantic attempts to hear his own playing during his years of deafness.

For nearly a hundred years Ludwig van Beethoven has been the most popular of the great composers. His music is played more often than that of any other composer, and his name is a household word.

The story of Beethoven's life, like that of J. S. Bach, is the story of his music. For the rest, it can be told very briefly. During the first seventeen years of his life he learnt music locally, and was sufficiently good at it to be asked to do quite important musical tasks in the district when he was only twelve. At seventeen he went to Vienna (we do not know why, or who paid for the trip) and caused a stir in musical circles with his piano-playing. During the three months of his stay he had a few lessons in composition from Mozart; but the two musicians did not get to know each other very well, though Mozart sensed Beethoven's genius. Back in Bonn, he continued writing music, rather slowly and painfully, and five years later a local nobleman sent him to Vienna again, at his own expense, for some more lessons. He never went back to Bonn.

So Beethoven, at the age of twenty-two, joined the great company of musicians who were making Vienna the centre of the art. Mozart had just died; Haydn was sixty, and at the height of his fame. Beethoven had some lessons from him, but they were not very successful; Haydn was pressed for time, and Beethoven would not do as he was told. When Haydn told him that certain chords were not allowed Beethoven said, "I allow them!" At this time he was rough, rude, independent, and full of music. But like many abrupt and independent people, he seemed to have an immense amount of charm which made him a favourite with many a noble family in Vienna. They arranged concerts for him, helped him to find pupils, and kept a roof over his head. Constantly they had to put up with his bad manners. "I'll not play for such hogs!" he once shouted when some one ventured to talk in the drawing-room while he was playing the piano; "*Fool* of a Lobkowitz!" he screamed at Prince Lobkowitz, his benefactor, when he got the arrangements wrong for a rehearsal. They all realized that among them was a great man; that this rough young man who played and composed was to be looked after and encouraged.

The rest of his story is well known. When he was about twenty-nine he began to hear strange buzzing noises; on a walk in the country he saw a shepherd playing a pipe and realized that he could not hear it. Deafness, the worst calamity for a musician, came fast upon him. It shut him off not only from the sound of his own music, but from people, and caused him to be even ruder and more suspicious of their behaviour than he was before. He never married, though he was several times in love, and his life was spent in one lodging after another in Vienna. He was afflicted with a waster of a nephew, who was constantly in trouble, and who used up a lot of the money Beethoven made out of his music.

Beethoven's answer to all these trials was to hit back. Though life dealt him blow after blow, he shouted his defiance. He died at the age of fifty-six at the height of a thunder-storm; his last action was to sit upright in bed and shake his clenched fist at the troubled sky.

That action is the key to Beethoven's music. It holds our attention because of its *power*. It is the power that is given only to those who are strong enough to go on living and creating beautiful things when everything that could make life beautiful for them has been snatched away.

Power in music does not mean mere noise; it does not depend on large blasts of sound. It is to be found in simple melodies:

Symphony No. 9 in D minor, by L. van Beethoven

Or in a mere handful of notes, which, like acorns, will grow into majestic oaks:

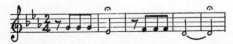

Symphony No. 5 in C minor, by L. van Beethoven

All Beethoven's music is driven along by a strong 'mainspring'; it compels our attention because it 'ticks' with such steadiness and such strength. Some of his compositions have been given nicknames which we all know. These were thought of by his publishers so that the works would sell more easily. If, in a future life, you were to meet Beethoven and mention the 'Moonlight' sonata to him he'd say, "I don't know what on earth you're talking about!" To Beethoven his music (with a very few exceptions) was just music. It was his way of pouring out his heart to all those who wished to listen. And the whole western world has listened and enjoyed for a hundred and fifty years.

No pianist in the whole world can work at the piano for more than a year without 'coming on to Beethoven.' From the sonatinas he passes to the sonatas, those wondrous thirty-two piano works which are the 'bread and butter' of all pianists, and which are a kind of chronicle of the composer's life. Through them the young pianist learns how to get his fingers (and his brain!) used to big music. He must begin each sonata saying to himself, "Once upon a time," and then he must proceed to tell his audience a lengthy and enthralling story, not of fairies or giants, but of *human beings*, and what happens to them. For all Beethoven's music is human; it mirrors the feelings of people, their happinesses and strivings, their yearnings and their ways of achieving them. Sometimes (in an early sonata, such as the *'Pathétique'*) one can almost hear the young Beethoven saying to us, "This is what *I* feel like! It is very important that you should hear about *my* emotions—they matter so much more than yours!" But when we get to the later sonatas we find his mood has changed. "There's nothing *really* so important about what I myself feel," he seems to say, "because I realize that I share my feelings with the whole world. My music describes the emotions of all people, not just my own." In his young days he would fling out a musical cry of self-pity like this:

Sonata in C minor, op. 13 ('Pathétique'),
by L. van Beethoven

Later he would begin a sonata with a simple phrase which seems to gather in the performer, the listener, and the whole world as well as the composer into the centre of its musical feeling:

P con amabilita

Sonata in A flat, op. 110, by L. van Beethoven

From the sonatas the pianist passes on to discover the five piano concertos. In these Beethoven's two favourite instruments, the piano and the orchestra, are brought together. The first two concertos show them getting on well together, as they did in Mozart's concertos; they 'consort' with each other, and dwell together in harmony. In the third concerto, however, their relations begin to be strained. The piano is heard putting up a heroic struggle against the orchestra. It is not trying to drown it, but simply to speak with the same force and power. Strife is also to be heard in the fourth concerto in G major, though here it seems to take place far above the earth, so swift and light of touch is the music. The fifth concerto (known everywhere as the 'Emperor') brings us right back into the world again. The huge march of the first movement, the noble, mellow conversation between piano and orchestra of the second, and the clod-hopping rustic dance of the third show us the solo instrument and the orchestra as mighty rivals, equal in strength. It is a strenuous contest, but a friendly one. In the slow movement tune we can see how carefully and painfully Beethoven wrote his music; he had at least three shots at this tune before he hammered it into shape:

The nine symphonies are perhaps the most powerful music ever written. It is in them that Beethoven's musical 'mainspring' is most tightly coiled. From the very first one it is obvious that the word 'symphony' has come to mean 'bigger' music than ever before. In the structure of the symphony Beethoven made an important change. He felt that the time was past for the third movement to consist of a cosy little aristocratic dance—a minuet and trio—so, keeping the same A-B-A shape, he would write a movement marked *Allegro molto e vivace* (very fast and lively) to take its place. This he called a *scherzo*, which means a 'joke.' There is nothing funny about Beethoven's scherzos, however; they are savage jokes.

Sometimes Beethoven had a particular idea in his mind when he wrote a symphony. The third, for instance, is known as the 'Eroica'; it was a tribute to Napoleon, whom, as a man, Beethoven admired very much. He was very disappointed when Napoleon set himself up as Emperor; he thought he was too great a man to be working towards such selfish ends. Beethoven crossed out the dedication to Napoleon and inscribed the slow movement (a funeral march), "To the memory of a great man." The sixth was called by Beethoven the *Pastoral*; it has sections called *By the Brook*, *The Storm*, and *Thanksgiving after the Storm*. The seventh, though it has not got a name, is a series of glorious dance-measures. The ninth is the first symphony to have a chorus and soloists in it; Beethoven, nearing the end of his unhappy life, gave proof of his courage against fearful odds by ending the symphony with a setting of Schiller's *Ode to Joy*, a shout of praise and optimism.

The most popular, and possibly the strongest and most impressive of the symphonies is the fifth. Perhaps this is because it has behind it Beethoven's strongest and most impressive idea: the ability of the human spirit to shake its fist at whatever troubles life might bring. The fifth is strength and courage in musical sound, and no one can hear it without feeling stronger and braver.

For the string-player there are the ten violin sonatas, the five cello sonatas, and, most important, the seventeen string quartets. The string quartet, after its journey through the years from Haydn and Mozart, was brought to a height of musical excellence by Beethoven, which it has never reached since. As in the case of the piano sonatas, Beethoven was writing string quartets throughout his life, and in them we can see how his style and his mood changed. The last quartets reach out into realms of music which cannot be visited by any but the most advanced and sensitive listeners and players; they are visionary works.

In vocal music Beethoven achieved less than in instrumental music. His one opera, *Fidelio*, caused him more trouble than any other of his works. His finest choral music (the *Missa Solennis* and the last movement of the Ninth Symphony) makes such heavy demands on the voices that many people find it too uncomfortable to enjoy. Beethoven's vision was so blinding that he did not pause to consider whether what he wrote was within the power of mere human singers. Nevertheless, the Mass is one of the great choral works. The solo songs, also written very painfully, mark a step forward in songwriting, but no more than that; living a few streets away from Beethoven was a young composer who was to do for that branch of music what Beethoven did for the piano and the orchestra.

It was in sonata form that Beethoven's finest musical thoughts grew. C. P. E. Bach had groped towards it:

Haydn gave it a firm outline; Mozart refined it and polished it. Now Beethoven came to make it grow in the power to express feeling.

Beethoven was, once again, the right man at the right time. Palestrina had brought polyphonic church music to its peak; J. S. Bach had gathered up all the musical threads of the past eighty years and had woven them into a richer cloth than ever before. Beethoven took what was by now quite an old bottle—sonata form—and filled it with new and heady wine.

When Beethoven was twenty-seven Franz Schubert was born in Vienna. He lived only thirty-one years, and in his short working life left us so many beautiful tunes that it is impossible to think about 'tunes' in music without thinking of Schubert. His life, like Beethoven's, can be told in a few sentences. He was a schoolmaster's son. At an early age he showed that he was full of music, and had the good fortune to sing his way into the Imperial Choir School. Here, besides the singing, there was orchestral training and lessons in composition, so that the rather timid bespectacled little boy with a beautiful voice was surrounded by the music he needed. In due course he became a teacher in his father's school, taking the lowest class, and scribbling his music in spare moments. Only two more things need to be mentioned: his stay for a few years in Hungary, and his capacity for friendship. In 1818 (when he was twenty-one) he was engaged to teach the daughters of Count Johann Esterhazy (the name we remember so well in connexion with Haydn), and left Vienna for the Esterhazys' country house in Hungary. Before and after his journey (the only one he ever made) he was looked after and encouraged year after year by student friends of his own age, who saw to it that he had a roof over his head and something to eat, that he was supplied with music paper day and night, and that his music was heard by as many people as possible. They gave him many an affectionate nickname; the nicest one was 'Kanervas.' Whenever his friends introduced him to a new member of their circle his first question was, "Kann er was?" ("Can he do anything?") So we do not think of Schubert in a large concert-hall, an impressive figure before a clamorous audience. He gave only one public concert in his life, and he never heard a note of any of his large orchestral works—not even the 'Unfinished' Symphony. We must think of him as sitting at the piano in a drawing-room, with his close friends gathered round him, playing and singing his newest song for their delight. Before his early death he "found time," as one writer has said, "to leave with us countless beautiful melodies as he passed by."

In many ways Schubert helped to make musical history to a greater extent than any composer since Haydn. As we have seen, most of the great composers happened to write their music at a time when they could sum up the work that certain other composers had done before them, and, in doing so, carry it to a higher level than it had reached before. Schubert, although he loved Mozart's music and lived under the very shadow of Beethoven, looked into the future, like a prophet. Though he wrote sonatas, symphonies and string quartets in sonata form, he was not so interested in the working-out of his ideas as in the sheer *sound* of them. He revelled in beautiful tunes and harmonies, and in dramatic changes from one mood to another. He would repeat a beautiful tune two or three times because it sounded beautiful; if the whole piece was rather long as a result it did not matter to him. It was to be only a few years before most composers were going to think that sound, drama, and 'sound-painting' were the only things that mattered in music. The Romantic period was beginning, and Schubert was caught on the fringe of it.

Every one knows a Schubert tune. None of us passes through school without learning *Hark, hark, the Lark,* or *Who is Sylvia?* or *Rose among the Heather.* They are tunes which come so easily to us that we are often inclined to forget that they sprang from the pen of a composer. They seem, like Topsy, to have just growed. Schubert spent his whole working life in the grip of composition. Music paper must always be at hand—he used to sleep with his spectacles on in case some tune came to him during the night. He seemed to be nothing more than a channel through which music flowed like fresh, clear water.

Just as a bull is said to be goaded into action by the sight of a red rag, so was Schubert by the reading of a poem! Any poem he came across, good or bad, caused him to dash down on paper some music to fit it. The tune and the piano accompaniment work together to take us right to the kernel of the poem's meaning. Often, with poor words, a simple tune, and an accompaniment with hardly any notes in it, Schubert can paint a most vivid picture. It might be a desperate lover meeting a hurdy-gurdy man in an icy street in winter, or a young girl at her spinning-wheel, thinking of her lover so intensely that she forgets to keep her wheel turning. A later composer, Robert Schumann, once said that "Franz Schubert could have set a poster to music!" Whereas some composers (including Beethoven) found words a nuisance when they were writing music, Schubert found them his main inspiration. He is still the finest writer of songs that has ever been; no one has been able to improve on him.

If you sing his songs in class you do not hear them at their best. They need to be sung by a solo voice (by a thoroughly trained singer) and accompanied by a most intelligent pianist. They are not just tunes with an accompaniment; they are duets, with both members of the team on equal terms. They are known by a special name—*Lieder*. This is merely the German word for 'songs,' but a *Lied* is a song in which there is this close partnership between singer and pianist, which is necessary to convey what Schubert was trying to tell us in his songs. Sometimes he links several *Lieder* together to make a story. In the twenty songs which go to make up *The Maid of the Mill*, for instance, we follow the fortunes of a young miller. He sets out to seek work, and follows a brook because it will lead him to a mill-wheel; he finds his mill, and falls in love with the miller's daughter. Soon she deserts him in favour of a huntsman dressed in green; green becomes the miller's hated colour, but rather than attempt to escape from it he drowns himself in the brook, which murmurs his last good-bye. It is a silly story, and told in rather second-rate poetry. Schubert's endlessly beautiful music, however, makes us think that we are listening to the unfolding of a great love-story. From the jaunty opening song, "To wander is the miller's joy"— you must have sung it—through the great happiness of his love, the stinging jealousy, the despair, to the brook's final farewell, the changing moods are matched with the most sensitive music, and through it all can be heard the rippling brook. Then there is *The Winter Journey*, a group of twenty-four songs which describes the sufferings of a forsaken lover, wandering heartbroken from place to place in the winter's cold. Such groups of songs are called *song cycles*. They were not Schubert's invention—Beethoven and lesser men had written some before—but it is Schubert's song cycles which have inspired every later composer of songs to try his hand at them.

Songs with piano, trios, string quartets and quintets, small choral pieces, piano sonatas—Schubert could hear and perform all these with the help of his devoted musical friends. The nine large symphonies, needing a good orchestra, were just heard by his mental ear; he was not sufficiently well-known to get them into concert programmes. There was one way, however, in which he could write large music so that he could hear it; he could spread it out as a piano duet (four hands on the one keyboard). This he often did, and he has left us some magnificent music for two good pianists to play. In the *Grand Duo*, the Fantasy in F minor, the Variations in A flat, and the *Hungarian Rondo* we can find some of his richest music, and though we often feel that they cry out for the sound of orchestral instruments, we can revel in their melodious sweetness and poetry as they come to life under our fingers.

Of the nine symphonies the most frequently played are the fifth in B flat, the eighth in B minor, and the ninth in C; the most popular, of course, is the eighth—the 'Unfinished.' This consists of only two movements instead of the usual four, and there are only a few bars of the third movement, the *Scherzo*. We do not know why he did not finish it, though there have been many guesses; it is most likely that some event interrupted him at that point, and when he was ready to take it up again some new idea had filled his mind. As it stands, however, it is in a different world from Beethoven's symphonies—a world of sudden moods and glorious flights of fancy, long melodies and temperamental outbursts. In a Beethoven symphony we can hear a massive, powerful piece of mechanism swinging into motion; in one by Schubert we seem to be tapping a mountain spring. This difference causes many people to think of Schubert as a 'feminine Beethoven'; for them, music which relies on sound and tune is weaker than music which relies largely on rhythm and form. It is far better to think of the two composers as completely separate from each other, though they did live at the same time and in the same place. Beethoven is on the top of a mountain peak, looking back at the country behind him, with only an occasional glance into the land in front of him; Schubert has already passed forward, and, with the peak behind him, is looking forward into the misty, uncertain artistic world that lies ahead.

What was this world? It was a new one, and it was created by new ways of thinking that were sweeping over Europe. It expressed itself in a new kind of literature, painting, and music; in politics it gave rise to the French Revolution. This world was coming into being while Mozart was writing his music; Beethoven stood on the threshold of it; Schubert wandered right into it. It was a world in which all people were to be free, equal, and at peace with each other. In the political world it meant revolution; in the artistic world it led to the throwing overboard of all the old rules, and an urge to express one's own feelings at any price! The world of ordinary people was too dull; artists and musicians and writers reached out to fairy-tales—ghosts, witches, demons, giants, all became important. Corpses, graveyards at midnight, the devil on a stormswept mountain-top, all loomed large in the imaginations of these "free, equal, and peaceful" people. For a composer it was no longer enough merely to compose; he had to look like a composer and behave like one. The world had to be able to point at him and say, "There goes a genius!" Art of all kinds became as much a part of the artist as his odd-looking clothes, his glittering eye, his pallid cheeks, and his early death or madness.

The Romantic era had begun.

The Dawn of the Romantic Era

WE have been dealing with four musical giants: Haydn, Mozart, Beethoven, and Schubert. They all lived in one city, Vienna, and their music was written within, roughly, eighty years (1750 to 1830), the mere lifetime of many a healthy person nowadays.

Once again our historical beam of light shines so strongly on Vienna (as it once did on Rome and London) that our eyes are too dazzled to be able to pick out other places and people. In fact, however, nothing much *was* happening anywhere else—though it is the last time one is able to say this. Only towards the end of this time, when the Romantic era was dawning, was there an important move forward in the art of music.

To fill in the outlines of our historical shape we need only sketch in three patterns, which we can call Keyboard, Opera, and Programme Music.

From Harpsichord to Piano

The change-over from quills plucking strings to hammers hitting them was a gradual one. Experiments had been going on for a long time, but the first man to make a piano which 'came to stay' was an Italian, Bartolomeo Cristofori, who produced a *fortepiano* (as the pianoforte was called in its early days) in 1720. An instrument of this type soon found its way into the Bach family. J. S. Bach said its tone was too rough and its keys too heavy; of his musical sons, C. P. E. said it was "only fit for rondos," but J. C., who settled in London, took to it and wrote excellent music for it. Both Haydn and Mozart played the piano, but, according to reports, they played it as if they were playing the harpsichord; that is to say, they did not take advantage of the extra smoothness and linking of notes that was possible only on the piano. By the time Beethoven had begun to write his piano sonatas several lesser men had taken to the piano as an expressive musical instrument. The sonatinas of Muzio Clementi (1752–1832) and Friedrich Kuhlau (1786–1832) showed Beethoven how the tone of a piano could be kept on through several notes by means of the right-hand pedal, and how a 'singing tune' could be played by the same means. The English firm of Broadwood made him a gift of one of their most advanced models. Schubert, as we have seen, used the piano for nearly all his music; he tried out his orchestral effects on it, as its tone was so much richer and varied than that of the harpsichord. The piano was now established as a popular and useful instrument; soon someone was going to write music which revealed its poetic soul—Frédéric Chopin.

Opera

We left opera with Mozart. Beethoven wrote one opera, *Fidelio*, which is full of majesty and deeply felt, but not quite successful as drama; Schubert wrote quite a number of them, but the words and the stories which he chose prevented them from becoming well known.

It was in opera that the new Romantic spirit first showed itself. Mozart, in *Don Giovanni*, built his story round a supernatural happening; a stone statue comes to life and causes Hell to open and swallow up the hero. In *The Magic Flute* there are mysterious figures: serpents, wild animals, and two young people in search of wisdom, truth, and love. Then came a German composer who, in three operas, stepped right into the Romantic world. This was Carl Maria von Weber (1786–1826). In 1821 he produced an opera called *Der Freischütz* (*The Marksman*). The story deals with a forester who, in order to win a shooting contest, is shown by another forester how to mould some magic bullets which cannot miss their target.

The scene of the forging of these bullets is the Wolf's Glen, at midnight. It is the most eerie scene in the whole of opera. As each of the six bullets is cast horrific things happen on the stage:

> *One!* Night birds swoop down upon the greenish flames of the crucible. . . .
>
> *Two!* A black boar crashes through the bushes and darts wildly across. . . .
>
> *Three!* A hurricane rises, breaking the tops of the trees. . . .
>
> *Four!* A rattling of wheels, cracking of whips, and horses. Four wheels darting fire roll across the stage. . . .
>
> *Five!* Neighing and barking, misty forms of hunters; stags and hounds rush through the air. . . .
>
> *Six!* Thunder, lightning, and hail; flames start from the earth; meteors appear on the hills. . . .

Bells tolling, illuminated skulls, fearful, ghostly echoing voices, all combine to make one's hair stand on end. Thus did the Romantic era descend on the Germans. No longer did their art say to us, "These are my great thoughts, and those of all people"; it now said, "This is what I feel, and that is all that matters."

A healthier air was blowing through Italian opera. Its chief composer during this time was Gioachino Rossini (1792–1868), who, after writing no fewer than thirty-six operas in nineteen years, virtually retired at the age of thirty-seven, and lived a lazy life on the money they brought in. Most of his operas were staged in either Italy or France, but in 1822 he brought some of them to Vienna, where their great success made the conceited Viennese musicians furious. But his sparkling melodies and his full-blooded effects made a vivid impression on the Viennese composers. Weber, Schubert, and even Beethoven found themselves influenced by his music. In return, Rossini learnt a good deal from them about the use of large orchestral masses of sound, and the 'symphonic' building of movements. While in Vienna, Rossini paid a call on Beethoven, who said to him, "Don't waste time writing serious music, but give us plenty of 'Barbers.'" *The Barber of Seville* is Rossini's most popular opera; in fact it is the only one which is regularly to be seen in opera houses today. Strangely enough, it was a complete failure when it was first staged; Rossini's fame used to rest on his serious works. But Beethoven proved to be right.

Programme Music

Most people, when they begin to listen to music, ask, "What is the story behind it?" They expect music to be always *describing* something which has nothing to do with music—galloping horses, the setting sun, the sea beating against the rocks, or even a man being buried alive. If you tell them that there's no "story behind it" they say it is "above their heads," or "too heavy," or that they "can't appreciate it." It takes them a long time to realize that most of the great music of the world is—just music, that it is sound, and mood, and shape. Music cannot paint pictures or tell stories; it can only *suggest* them.

You can, however, cause people to see pictures and stories in music, *if you tell them what these are beforehand*. It was pointed out in the last chapter, for instance, that Beethoven's Sixth Symphony is 'about' something; he has given it a title (*Pastoral*) and some headings for the movements which tell us what he had in his mind when he wrote the music. If you give a piece of music a name, such as *The Windmill*, or *By the Lake*, it is bound to suggest a picture to the listener before he hears a note of the music, and then he will see that picture in sound. Though several of the early composers called some of their music by names (François Couperin (1668–1733) wrote some delightful keyboard pieces with such names as *The Jugglers*, *The Princess*, and *The Cuckoo*, and Johann Kuhnau (1660–1722) told bible-stories in music

(*The Fight of David and Goliath*)) most of the great composers were content to give their works titles such as 'Sonata in E flat,' or 'Symphony No. 5 in C minor,' or 'Pianoforte Concerto No. 4 in G,' and to leave the listener to find his own musical pleasure in them.

But now came the Romantic Movement, with all its vivid imaginings and its stormy feelings. The Romantic composers were compelled to put these into music, but how could the listeners tell what they were? How terrible it would be if people got these feelings and imaginings wrong! They must be described at the beginning of the music in words, so that there could be no mistake about them! So it came about that a French composer, Hector Berlioz (1803–69), wrote a great symphony which was called, not 'Symphony in C minor,' but *Fantastic Symphony—Episodes in the Life of an Artist*; and the separate movements were not only headed *allegro*, *andante*, or with any of the usual words which show the speed and the mood of the music, but also

1. *Dreams—Passions*
2. *A Scene at a Ball*
3. *A Scene in the Country*
4. *March to the Scaffold*
5. *Dream of a Witch's Sabbath*

The listener is left in no doubt as to what was going on in Berlioz's mind while he was writing the work—but that does not make the music either better or worse.

Through Berlioz the centre of the Romantic Movement shifted to France. It was already raging there among the authors and poets—Alexandre Dumas was writing his novels, Victor Hugo his soulful poems and daring plays. Sir Walter Scott and Lord Byron were busy in England with their tales of chivalry, witchcraft, and the sufferings of romantic youths in search of something they knew not what; but English music was still silent. In Germany Goethe was exploring the character of the Devil in his plays, and Weber, as we have seen, was putting Black

Magic on the operatic stage. Only Italy was keeping free of the Romantics.

This new feeling in music is now about to spread itself over the historical scene through a whole cluster of famous composers. They nearly all wrote their best music for the piano. So that we shall not become thoroughly confused by all these great names, and so lose our way along the historical path, we will divide them up like this:

1. Composers who broke away from the classics and followed the new romantic path: Liszt, Schumann, Chopin.

2. Those who had the new Romantic ideas, but who tried to fit them into the classical forms of sonata, symphony, and concerto: Mendelssohn, Brahms.

3. The composers of opera: Wagner, Verdi.

It is easy to remember *when* they wrote their music, as they all fit nicely into two 'slabs' of time:

    1. The first half of the 1800's:

        Chopin (1810–49)
        Mendelssohn (1809–47)
        Schumann (1810–56)

    2. The second half of the 1800's:

        Brahms (1833–97)

    3. Spread across the whole century:

        Liszt (1811–86)
        Wagner (1813–83)
        Verdi (1813–1901)

8

New Paths—The Romantic Era

WE know the sound of music of the 1800's better than that of any other period. We hear it as background music in the cinema, as favourite hymns in church, as popular ballet music and musical comedy on the stage. It seems to us to be music's natural language; any earlier music seems to belong to the past, and any later music seems to be 'modern,' with wrong notes in it here and there. If we try to make up a tune, or if we allow our fingers to wander about on the keyboard, the sounds we make are usually those of the music of Chopin, Liszt, or Mendelssohn. The reason for this may be that the Romantic composers, as we have seen, tried all the time to express personal feelings; they did not concern themselves with the Nobility of Man, or the Majesty of God, or any other great, universal theme. They portrayed their own yearnings and moods, whether these were important to the rest of the world or not, and as we all share the same moods we like to hear them described in musical sound.

Of all the 'mood-composers' the most important in any history of music are Schumann and Liszt.

Robert Schumann was the son of a bookseller. As a boy he was already reading as much as he could of the new Romantic literature—the German works of Heine and Goethe, the mad, fantastic stories of Hoffmann, the poems of Byron, the novels of Sir Walter Scott, and, above all, the deeply emotional poems of Jean Paul, which he discovered when he was seventeen. He studied law (against his will), tried hard to be a concert pianist (but had to give it up because of a crippled finger), edited a musical journal, married a young concert pianist, Clara Wieck, in spite of parental opposition, poured out his happiness in glorious songs and piano music, and finally died in a mental home after a long illness. By far the most important event in his life was his marriage to Clara Wieck. She was an ideal partner. Through her brilliant piano-playing she was able to introduce his music to audiences as he himself, with his crippled finger, could not do, and by her love for him, and his for her, she inspired him to write such beautiful and warm-hearted songs as *Devotion, The Walnut Tree*, and *Thou art like a Flower*. She lived until almost the end of the century, and played and taught her husband's music to several people who are still alive to-day.

If Schumann's life was outwardly unexciting his inner one was that of a true Romantic. His impulsive, restless mind was constantly at work creating not only music, but imaginary people. In his articles on music he used to divide himself into three: as 'Florestan' he was a young, eager student; as 'Eusebius' he was a thoughtful, careful thinker; and as 'Meister Raro' he was a kind of chairman, keeping them both in order. He even formed a secret society, called the 'Davidsbündler,' whose members met, elected new members, discussed new music, and kept minutes of their meetings. As one of the members was Mozart (who had died just over forty years before) it was obvious that this society only existed in Schumann's imagination! Many of its members found their way into his music, however, and we meet some of them in one of his most magical piano works: *Carnaval*.

Schumann's music is very much a part of the man himself; when one plays it one often feels as if one is talking with the composer on any subject under the sun—warmly, affectionately, changing from one thing to another, as close friends do when they meet. Schumann hardly ever makes speeches; he never shouts from the housetops. There is never any need for the pianist to pounce on his keyboard like a tiger; singers do not have to scream high notes or rush up and down the scale; orchestras need not crowd the concert-platforms with noisy extra instruments. It has been said of his beautiful Piano Concerto that it was "written by candlelight"; this is just the right description of Schumann's music. It deals with moods, not pictures or stories. When he wrote his suite of poetic little pieces called *Scenes from Childhood* he added the titles *after* he had written the music. "The names," he said, "are merely *delicate suggestions* to the player as to how the music should be played." So that when we play, for instance, *An Important Event* we find ourselves trying to make the large, pompous chords sound like a brass band playing at the head of a procession through the town; and in *The Child falling Asleep* we use a drowsy, caressing touch on the piano—at the change of key we can imagine a pleasant memory of the day's happenings stirring the child on the point of sleep, and finally, in the last phrase, finishing before it has got us back to the main key, the child fading into deep slumber. . . .

Schumann wrote four symphonies, a good deal of chamber music, concertos for violin, cello, and piano, and an opera. His first and strongest love, however, was for the piano, and it is in works which include a piano that we find him at his best. In the Piano Concerto, the Piano Quintet, the songs, and the many fanciful collections of piano music we are able to meet the real Schumann—impulsive, warm-hearted, whimsical, and wholly lovable.

In 1811 a bright comet was seen in the sky over Europe, and in that year Franz Liszt was born in Hungary. Of course, there is no connexion between these two events, but there might well have been. For half a century Liszt dominated Europe as a pianist, a composer, and a man; travelling continuously through his orbit of Rome, Paris, London, Weimar, Budapest, he electrified audiences with his playing, brought the whole of aristocratic society to his feet, fascinated all musicians from

Beethoven downward, and left behind him a glowing trail of adoration.

He has been called the greatest pianist that has ever lived. This he may or may not have been; much of his piano music is very difficult to play, and until a few years ago some of it was thought to be impossible for anyone to play but Liszt himself. By now, however, so much more has been learnt about how our muscles work when we play the piano that present-day students are not unduly troubled by the great technical difficulties of his music. In any case, Liszt's playing died with him, and it is on his compositions that we have to base our estimate of his importance in musical history. Whether we like his music or not, he *is* an important musician, as he has altered the course of music in several ways.

Let us divide up his work thus:

1. Piano music.
2. Orchestral music.
3. Transcription (*i.e.*, changing other kinds of music —symphonies, songs, operas—into piano solos).

The only three 'classical' piano works of any importance are the two concertos and the Sonata in B minor. Otherwise all Liszt's piano music is true Romantic music —there is a scene, or a story, or a mood. There are collections of piano pieces with such names as *Years of Pilgrimage* (in which we hear *The Fountains of the Villa d'Este* or *The Bells of Geneva*), and there are *Transcendental Studies* (written to test out pianists' sinews and fingers), called by such titles as *Will o' the Wisp* and *The Wild Huntsman*. Countless other pieces with fanciful names show us that Liszt really needed something outside music to cause him to begin to compose. All his piano music uses the whole keyboard from top to bottom. Never before had people realized how many notes pianists could use, how quickly they could move about on the keyboard, and what rich and exciting sounds they could make on it. Though he spent hardly any time in Hungary he gave the country of his birth a musical salute by writing fifteen *Hungarian Rhapsodies*, using Hungarian folk-tunes as a basis for incredibly brilliant piano-gymnastics.

> The Abbé Liszt
> Played the piano with his fist;
> That is the way
> He used to play.

That is what an English humorist once said about him; it is not a good advertisement for Liszt's playing, but it indicates the sort of sound he made when he played—louder, faster, and more exciting than that made by any pianist before.

During one of his visits to Paris Liszt heard Victor Hugo read some of his poems. As the poetry unfolded Liszt's mind began to turn it into music. So he brought into being a new form of music: the *symphonic poem*. It is, of course, a form of *programme music*. "Let the listener," said Liszt, "make himself acquainted with the poem before he hears the music, so that he may be on guard against receiving false impressions." But it does not merely tell the story of the poem in music; it *translates* the poetry into musical sound, just as you translate Latin into English. A famous critic puts it thus: "Instead of trying to tell us in music what the poet has already told us in verse, Liszt *rethinks* in music what the poet has already said, and gives it out to us as something born of musical feeling itself." Let us take an example. Liszt's most popular symphonic poem is called *Les Préludes*, and it is based on a poem by Lamartine which can be expressed in English like this:

> What is our life but a series of Preludes to an as yet unknown song, whose first notes are sounded by Death? We all start our journey in the magical dawn of love; but who has not known the time when all this is shattered by disaster; and when this happens, who does not yearn to seek comfort in the tranquillity of Nature's woods and fields? Yet no man is content to

stay there. When the trumpet sounds, he hastens back to the scene of his struggle, for only there is he really contented.

How does Liszt "rethink" that into music? First he maps out the main ideas in the order in which they appear in the poem:

1. The magical Dawn.
2. Tempest and Disaster.
3. Tranquillity of Nature.
4. The Trumpet Call to Action.
5. Victory.

Then, to turn these into music, he thinks of three tunes, or themes:

A. A large tune to express the whole noble idea of the poem.

B. A tender theme to suggest the "magical dawn of love."

C. A solid tune to suggest the strong and serene background of Nature.

Notice that he does not give each section of the poem a tune to itself and then string them all together to make a 'descriptive piece.' Using these three tunes, he causes them to change their *mood* (not their notes) as the ideas in the poem change. For instance, tune A returns at the end, greatly swollen up, to denote "Victory"; tune B is caused to seethe and boil to suggest the "Tempest and Disaster"; and tune C reappears as a stirring march for the "Trumpet Call to Action." In fact the main ideas of the poem are given *labels* (in the shape of tunes), and as those ideas change in *mood*, so do the tunes attached to them. Just as a dance-band often has a 'signature-tune' which you hear whenever it starts to play, so, in a symphonic poem, do the main ideas of the poet have their 'signature-tunes.' In music these are called 'leading motifs' ('leading tunes'), from the German word *leitmotiv,* and they become more and more important in the writing of music (and the listening to it) from Liszt onward.

The symphonic poem, then, is a sort of symphony in one movement, with these differences:

1. The music is inspired by something outside it, *e.g.,* a poem.
2. The tunes are not 'first and second subjects,' but a series of 'leading motifs,' each expressing a mood or an idea.
3. Instead of a 'development' of the first and second subjects there are 'transformations' of the 'leading motifs' to fit the various changes of mood in the poem or the story.

This new pattern, drawn by Liszt, became a great favourite with composers in the Romantic era, and it is still followed by all the leading composers to-day. It has been described at some length here because it led to very important changes in musical composition—especially in opera, as we shall see later.

Liszt's rethinking of poems leads to another sort of rethinking he did in music. To give himself more varied pieces to play to his adoring audiences, he 'arranged' an enormous amount of other composers' music for the piano. Schubert songs, Beethoven symphonies, Italian operas—all of these he 'transcribed' industriously for the piano keyboard. In the days before gramophone records and radio pianists were thus able to get to know the great orchestral and operatic music of past times through their fingers—*if* they could manage the frantically difficult passages that Liszt gave them to play! In his transcriptions Liszt did not just write down what the composer wrote; he rethought the works he was transcribing as a pianist would, with great numbers of extra 'twiddles' of the kind which pianists love to play, and which are so much a part of Liszt's style.

Liszt, then, was a towering historical figure in the

1800's, whatever we may think of his music now. As a person he was a strange mixture; at one moment he was enjoying every minute of his fame as a pianist and at the next he was in a monastery, studying to become a priest (he did eventually become one), thoroughly tired of showing off, and feeling guilty about it too. In the same way, generous person that he was, he felt all the time that he should help other composers as much as he could. He taught promising pianists free of charge, and no composer was turned away. He was more popular with audiences all over Europe than anyone has ever been since—even film-stars or crooners; he was a musical 'lion,' and at the same time a new kind of composer and a generous, open-hearted man.

It is not easy to realize how strong a hold the Romantic Movement had on Europe, especially upon artists. It was hardly possible to write, paint, or compose without becoming caught up in it. It must have been like a glorious summer, when, even if you do not like the hot weather much, you feel you must work, eat, and sleep in the open air, wear summer clothes (even if they don't fit), and feed on cool salads (which you may not particularly like).

Just at the time when Schumann and Liszt were looking into the future in their music there came two composers who looked into the past: Mendelssohn and Brahms.

Felix Mendelssohn-Bartholdy, the son of a rich banker, was one of the few composers who did not have to write for money, or who did not live in constant fear that they might starve. He began to write music at a very early age; one of his finest works, the overture to *A Midsummer Night's Dream*, was written when he was seventeen. And in this overture we can see immediately the difference between Mendelssohn's music and that of his fellow-Romantics, Schumann and Liszt. It deals, of course, with the characters in Shakespeare's play—the lovers, the Duke and the Queen, Bottom with his donkey's head, and, above all, the fairies in the "Wood near Athens." But if you lay this overture next to one by Mozart or Beethoven you will see that Medelssohn is using precisely the same shape or pattern as they used to use. *But*, at the same time, Mendelssohn speaks to us in the Romantic language; you can see the fairies, and you can almost *hear* Bottom braying stupidly and clumsily through his donkey's head.

Mendelssohn belonged to both worlds, the Classical and the Romantic, but he was better at the classical part of his work (that is, the shape of it) than at the romantic part (the setting-down of his moods and imagination in music).

But he too, like the other Romantic composers we have been talking about, did a great service to musical history —by looking back into the past and rediscovering the music of the greatest composer, Johann Sebastian Bach! You will remember from Signpost 2 that Bach's music was out of fashion even when he was still alive. And, until Mendelssohn appeared, composers had not shown any interest in music of the past hundred years. Even if Mendelssohn had not written a note of music of his own he would still be a most important figure in music because of his efforts to re-introduce Bach's choral music after it had been forgotten about since 1750. It was just as if a modern writer of plays had suddenly discovered *Hamlet* or *King Lear*, and had put them on the stage at a London theatre.

Mendelssohn tried to copy the style of Bach. He wrote oratorios, such as *Elijah* and *St Paul*, in which he tried to build up great masses of sound in counterpoint; he wrote sonatas for the organ with fugues in them, also in imitation of Bach. But, beautiful as they are, they have not got the staying-power of Bach. Mendelssohn was a *neat* composer, not a powerful one. When he writes about the sea (as he did in his lovely overture, *Fingal's Cave*) it is as if he were looking at it from the port-hole of a comfortable first-class cabin, rather than tossing about on it in an open boat, in fear of his life.

Mendelssohn was a great favourite in England. Queen Victoria liked the dapper little man, and approved of his music. She and Prince Albert used to sing his songs and play his charming *Songs without Words* on the piano. His oratorios, especially *Elijah*, were sung (and still are) by choral societies all over this country; they are colourful and utterly respectable, and do not require the singers to put themselves to a great deal of trouble either to sing them or to understand them.

He could write a good tune; his harmonies were just what people were used to in church when they sang *Hymns Ancient and Modern*; he gave pianists music to play which was cosily exciting or sentimental, and which needed neat and strong fingers to cope with its busy scales and octaves.

At his best he has a lightness of touch which, as one writer has said, "brings fairyland into the concert-hall." When we hear the *Midsummer Night's Dream* music, or the Octet, or the Violin Concerto we revel in the lightness and grace and beauty of the music just as we love a neat, formal garden, with its shapely lawns and flower-beds. There is magic in it.

England still had not produced a great composer; those who were writing music at that time felt that they could do nothing better than imitate Mendelssohn. From him they learned a most important part of their job—craftsmanship. Even if they did not have much to say in their music, they learned to say it neatly, clearly, and without fuss.

A word of warning here. If we group Mendelssohn and Brahms together as two composers who looked back to the classical period in music we must be careful about dates. We must remember that in the year Mendelssohn died Brahms was just a fourteen-year-old boy, and had hardly begun to write music. He belongs to the latter half of the 1800's, not to the period of Schumann and Mendelssohn. But it is tidier, if we are going to think of music in terms of history, to think of Brahms and Mendelssohn as two composers who treated their music in the same way, and who had the same ideas about it.

Johannes Brahms was the most 'solid' and classically-minded of all the composers of the Romantic period. He played Bach every morning, "to wash my mouth out"; he wrote *Variations on a Theme of Haydn*; when he produced his First Symphony it was called by some people (not without cause) "Beethoven's Tenth"; he produced sets of *Lieder* as a direct follow-on from Schubert. He seemed to regard himself as the heir to the great Viennese composers; "the mantle of Beethoven enwrapped him." If he had been a second-rate composer he would have been a horrible bore, so closely did he follow the musical patterns of the old classical masters. But he was not; his musical mind was of first-rate quality, and his music *grew*, as Beethoven's did, like a great oak-tree.

All around him the Romantic music was flourishing; amid Schumann's mood-music and Liszt's picture-music Brahms settled down to produce sonatas, symphonies, variations, chamber music, and concertos just as if he had been living round the corner from Beethoven and Mozart in Vienna sixty years previously. But he could not escape the new music. The sound of it was in his bones; his tunes, his harmonies, and, above all, his moods, were those of his time. If we listen to any of his four towering symphonies, or to his massive piano concertos, we can hear the spirit of the age speaking—the same spirit that speaks to us through Schumann. Like Mendelssohn, he took his musical shapes from the past and filled them out with his present-day music; but his music was more powerful and more varied than Mendelssohn's. We listen to a Mendelssohn symphony feeling that we are hearing a procession of shapely, melodious tunes with exciting interludes; a Brahms symphony rivets our attention, tightens our nerves, and makes the blood flow faster through our veins.

Brahms and Schumann were great friends; when Schumann died his widow, Clara, and Brahms carried on the friendship throughout their lives. She guided him, criticized his work, and inspired him. Brahms's life, in fact, was full of friendships which helped his music to get known. When he was twenty he went on tour in North Germany with a Hungarian violinist who later introduced him to the greatest violinist of the day, Joseph Joachim. Joachim sent him along to Liszt, who was always ready to listen to young, promising musicians. It must have been an amusing meeting. The young Brahms brought a piano piece to show to Liszt, but was too nervous to play it himself. Liszt played it, and liked it so much that he proceeded to play Brahms some of his own music. This was the greatest compliment that any young musician could receive in those days—but when Liszt turned from the piano at the end he found Brahms fast asleep! This sturdy independence and complete lack of 'nonsense' was Brahms himself; it shone out in his relations with people (especially when the whole musical world around him was quarrelling about him and Wagner) and it lights up his music. Half the musicians of the time looked upon him as the only sane artist in a mad Romantic world, and the other half as a stick-in-the-mud who was holding up progress. Nowadays, looking back on those times, we see that he was the last composer to speak to us in the well-known, well-loved language of the great German school of composers, but at the same time he was using modern words and expressions in his musical speech.

He did not have much consideration for the people who were going to play and sing his music. A pianist, tackling the huge B flat Piano Concerto, finds himself faced with a sort of marathon race over which he meets fearsome obstacles in the form of handfuls of chords, leaps from one end of the keyboard to the other, and thundering octaves. The beautiful Violin Concerto was called "A concerto *against* the violin"; choruses and orchestras have to be very careful to see that they do not get their chords out of tune; singers have to work hard to find the perfect balance between their part and that of the piano. He is more often against the performer than with him. But there is not a singer or player in the world who is not ready to give all his skill and patience to Brahms's music; it is so fine and satisfying.

Brahms has brought us into the second half of the 1800's. Now we must step back again into the first half, to deal with a composer who, for most listeners, is their favourite of all the Romantic composers—Frédéric Chopin.

Why have we not dealt with him before? Why have we left him so late in this chapter? The answer (though it will need some explaining) is that he was Polish. He wrote a great deal of his music with his native land in mind.

Now, so far we have seen over and over again how the best music seemed to spring from one particular centre in Europe—London, Rome, Vienna, and so on. But there was nothing *national* about this music. Palestrina was not thought of as a composer of *Italian* music, or Purcell of *English* music, or Mozart of *Austrian* music. Music 'travelled' very easily from one country to another; its sounds made a universal language that people of all countries could understand and like.

But now we have come to a point in history when composers began to write music 'with an accent.' They began to take notice of the songs and dance-tunes which their peoples had sung and played for hundreds of years: their *folk-music*. They began to use these tunes and rhythms, and this caused them to speak the language of music with a French accent, or a Russian one, or a Hungarian one. We can all tell a Yorkshireman from a Londoner, or a Scotsman from a Welshman, because they speak English in their own different ways. The time was coming now when it was possible to recognize a composer's native land through the sound of his music, and Chopin was one of the very first composers to 'give himself away' by his accent. That is why we have left him until now—because he leads on to the next phase in musical history.

Chopin had a Polish mother and a French father; he spent half of his short life in Warsaw, and half in Paris. Poland was his real home, however, and although he left it as a young man, never to return, it was the most important place in the world to him. We all know his name as well as we know Beethoven's; we are used to hearing his Polonaises and Nocturnes day after day, and his Funeral March on solemn occasions. Every pianist longs to 'get on to Chopin' as soon as possible, and it is very rarely that we can go to a piano recital without hearing at least one piece of his.

The whole of his fame is built on piano music. He hardly wrote any other kind of music, and when he did it was hardly worth bothering about. He and his piano made one glorious musical instrument; when he thought about music his mind's eye saw the gleaming keyboard, and his mind's ear heard the rippling, crashing, soothing, exciting sound that the piano can make.

Chopin's early life followed a familiar pattern. His parents, humble people, saw that Frédéric was full of music, and put him under the best teacher in the district. He was playing the piano at concerts when he was eight, and at fourteen he went as a student to the Warsaw Conservatoire of Music. When he was twenty he set off on his first concert tour. He was presented with a casket of Polish earth which, nineteen years later, was to be sprinkled on his coffin. Soon after he had left Warsaw he heard that the Russians had occupied it, and poured out his grief in the great 'Revolutionary' Study. He arrived eventually in Paris, to find the French people equally distressed about the fate of the Poles, and he was received most warmly and sympathetically. But he soon realized that he would not be content with the life of a travelling concert pianist; there was more to be done. He had already caused a stir in Germany with his compositions; Schumann had heard them and, in his lovable generous way, had lost no time in writing an article about them in his musical paper. He began with the words, "Hats off, gentlemen! a genius!" Chopin began to do less and less piano-playing, and more and more composing. He settled in Paris because there he found the kind of people he liked to have around him—intelligent, artistic, and witty. Unlike Schumann, he was not much interested in the other arts; he read very little and was not greatly impressed by pictures. But he loved people—their characters, their moods, and their warm-heartedness. It is very important to keep this in mind when we think about his music. We shall not find any 'picture-music' or 'story-music' among it (though people *have* given fanciful names to several pieces), but we shall find it full of human feeling. When we play the Nocturnes, the Preludes, the Scherzos, and the Ballades we seem to hear our own inmost thoughts and feelings 'coming back to us' in sounds that are brave, tender, savage, sparkling, and melancholy in turn.

But all the time he was remembering his native land, Poland; he could hear the songs the Polish people sang, and he could see the dances they danced—especially the Mazurkas and Polonaises. These are both vigorous, lively dances; the Mazurka is rough and clod-hopping, and the Polonaise is bold and stately, to be danced by beautiful women and gallant officers in full ceremonial uniform. Chopin took them and breathed his own poetry into them. He used their rhythms, but he never meant his Mazurkas and Polonaises to be danced to; he composed them all as Polish poems. They breathe the spirit of the country. And here for the first time we have important music speaking with a strong local accent; we can say, "This music could only spring from one place in Europe—from Poland, the country in which its composer was born!"

Chopin was never very strong; for many people he is the perfect example of an artist of the Romantic period. He looked 'pale and interesting,' and he suffered from the most fashionable illness of the day, a weakness of the lungs. For a whole winter he was looked after by a formidable lady-novelist who wrote under a man's name—'Georges Sand.' She took Chopin to Majorca to try to nurse him back to health, but the experience nearly killed him. It was the most rainy winter in living memory; the local peasants did not like them, and Chopin had no time for people who were not civilized and witty talkers; their landlord drove them out of their rooms when he discovered that Chopin was ailing; Chopin's piano was seized by the Customs and kept for over a month. The visitors finally had to seek refuge in a monastery, where Chopin spent his days listening to the rain and watching the moisture dripping down the stone walls of his cell.

When he got back to Paris he felt he could no longer play at big public concerts, and for the next ten years his only audiences were his close friends, to whom he used to play in drawing-rooms. In 1848 this elegant life in Paris began to break up; the Revolution was making itself felt. Chopin came over to Britain, where the musicians in London and Edinburgh gave him a warm welcome. His tour ended with a stay at a Scottish laird's castle; and as the rain fell, and the mists descended densely on the countryside, his mind must have gone back to that wretched winter ten years ago. He returned to Paris a very sick man, and died the following year.

Schumann, Liszt, Mendelssohn, Brahms, Chopin—these were the composers who put the new mood—the Romantic mood—into music. And yet they all did much more for music than that; each of them helped it to develop and become richer.

SCHUMANN discovered new composers and helped them to make their way. He also found a good deal of Schubert's music which had been overlooked, including the 'Great' C major Symphony, one of the favourite symphonies of all time.

LISZT explored the piano keyboard to its fullest extent, and showed just how much control a player's ten fingers have over it. He invented a new musical pattern, the symphonic poem, in which he linked up music and poetry more closely than they had ever been linked before.

MENDELSSOHN brought the music of J. S. Bach out of the shadows, and caused an immense wave of enthusiasm for it to break over Europe. To-day music without Bach would be like the stage without Shakespeare.

BRAHMS, surrounded by composers who seemed to say, "The *sound's* the thing! Don't let us worry too much about the *pattern*," went back to the patterns of music as Beethoven used them, and filled them out with Romantic music. He kept music sane when it was in danger of slipping into chaos and madness, and at the same time he made his music speak to his hearers in the new language.

CHOPIN brought the songs and dances of his native land into the concert-hall. In basing his music on these, he linked music with *nationality*. He also explored the *poetic sound* that the piano (with its hammers hitting strings) was able to produce.

But all these composers did their best work for the concert-hall. Though Schumann wrote an opera, it was not of any note. Mendelssohn wrote incidental music to various plays, but his overtures, like *Fingal's Cave* and *Ruy Blas*, were just concert pieces, as they were not intended to be played to open a stage performance. These five composers hardly entered the world of footlights and grease-paint.

But there were two others who did. Both remarkable men, they closed the gap between music and the stage throughout the 1800's and made sure that opera, perhaps the most exciting form of music, was kept alive—and growing.

PAUSE

Most of the last chapter was concerned with piano music—which is not strange when we remember that three of the composers we dealt with (Liszt, Chopin, and Schumann) were all at one time concert pianists, and wrote music for themselves to play, and that the other two (Mendelssohn and Brahms) were occupied in keeping 'classical' music going in the concert-hall.

The orchestra was not neglected—far from it. In the hands of Berlioz (see Signpost 3) it grew bigger, louder, and yet more sensitive than it had ever been before. For the first time it seemed that a composer saw the orchestra not just as a sweet-voiced instrument to convey his musical ideas, but as a means of providing the richest possible sound-effects. Berlioz was a master of the orchestra; he could make it produce featherweight sounds, as in the *Dance of the Sylphs*, or ear-splitting salvoes of noise, as in his overtures. His head was full of new sound-effects. While he was thinking out one of them for a new overture he slipped and sprained his ankle. He said, "For a long time this music gave me a pain in my ankle when I heard it. Now it gives me a pain in the head."

Of our piano composers, all but Chopin wrote a good deal of music for the orchestra, but only Liszt followed up Berlioz's way of treating it. Mendelssohn, Schumann, and Brahms used the normal-sized orchestra—Mendelssohn neatly and clearly, Schumann in chunks of sound as if it were a piano, and Brahms with great power and mellowness.

But the new Berlioz orchestra lived and grew—in the orchestra-pit of the new opera-house.

9

Wagner and Verdi

OVER the nineteenth century there looms a towering musical giant. Richard Wagner crammed more work into his seventy years than any musician—or even any man has ever done. In any opera-house of any size in the world you can hear some or all of his best-known operas —*Tannhäuser, Lohengrin, The Flying Dutchman, The Mastersingers, Tristan and Isolde,* or *The Ring*; they come round year after year. Each opera is a full evening's listening; *The Mastersingers,* for instance, goes on for over five hours, and *The Ring,* consisting of four operas, needs four evenings! Now, this would not be so striking were it not that they were all completely 'one-man' shows. We find it difficult to believe that Wagner himself

wrote the music *and* the words,
designed the scenery and the dresses,
worked out the stage management and designed the machinery,
chose *and trained* the special kind of singers he needed,
toured the country raising money for the productions,
designed and built a special theatre for his operas.

When one sits hour after hour in Covent Garden, listening to the huge orchestra playing all the time and to the singers relating their immensely long stories; when one watches the flames leaping round Brünnhilde's funeral-pyre, or the War-Maidens wheeling through the sky, one wonders how the mind of any man was large enough to think of it all, or how he could find time to write it all down.

But although he did the work of half a dozen men in his lifetime it is not the *amount* of his work that makes him important in the history of music. Lots of composers have written enough music to sink a rowing-boat, but their names are not mentioned in this book because they could not write music which was good enough to last. Wagner's music is heard year after year because it is great music; listeners all over the world hear it and enjoy it.

Wagner came from a theatrical family, and spent a lot of his school-days in reading poetry and plays, and writing them himself. But music was going on inside his head too; it was not long before he was thinking of music, words, and drama as one big way of expressing himself. In Dresden, where he lived for a time, there often came to the house an exciting visitor—Weber, who wrote *Der Freischütz*, with its terrifying Wolf's Glen scene (p. 120). Here, right on Richard Wagner's doorstep, was the man who had actually written just the kind of music he dreamed about, and Weber became his hero. At the same time Richard was hearing Beethoven's music, and knew at once that he must try to write music like that himself to fit the great dramas he had in mind. So he found a book of rules and taught himself. Even then, at the age of about seventeen, he not only knew what he wanted to do, but he was quite certain that he could do it.

Though it was some time before the great dramas came to anything, it was clear to his parents that Richard must be trained as a musician. He did nothing to startle the musical world in his early days, as so many composers had done; by the time he was twenty-six he was known only as a bright young conductor and producer in a small opera-house. He was 'learning the ropes' as a composer of opera, but that was all.

But now he felt it was time to move, to take a risk. He would go to Paris, where, no doubt, he could beguile the authorities at the opera-house into putting on an opera he was busy with. They would immediately recognize him as a great genius, of course, and he would be the talk of Europe. So away they went—Wagner, his young wife, and an enormous Newfoundland dog—on a roundabout journey by sea, from a Baltic port. This was the first time Wagner had been on the sea, and it was a very rough crossing, so rough that it caused him to think of some wonderful 'sea-music' which later became the overture to *The Flying Dutchman*. The Wagners landed first in London, and stayed for a few days. They knew nobody, and spent their time in sightseeing. Finally, with letters of introduction to important people in his pocket, he arrived in Paris. Alas for his brave plans! All the important people were polite and most friendly: they promised him engagements as a conductor and producer of operas; they said they were anxious to see some of his own work with a view to arranging performances. But *two years later* all that Paris had heard of Wagner's music was one short orchestral piece! For all their friendliness the Parisians obviously looked upon Wagner as a rash, conceited young German (which indeed he was), and quietly ignored him. During this time he and his wife lived in miserable lodgings; Wagner got odd jobs as a music copyist and also arranged a good deal of other people's music for different groups of instruments. He even tried to get a job as a member of the chorus in a small theatre, but, as he told his wife, "The conductor who tested me found out that I could not sing at all; in fact he wrote me off as a hopeless musician!"

Soon there was nothing to do but go back to Germany. It was not so depressing a prospect as it might have been because, after a great deal of delay, the opera-house at Dresden (where Wagner had lived for a time as a child) accepted his first important opera, *Rienzi*. It was a great success, and Wagner's fortunes had changed for the time being. He was able to write his operas with the fair chance that they would find their way on to the stage. *Rienzi* was followed by *The Flying Dutchman*, and then by *Tannhäuser*. By that time he had been appointed conductor at the opera-house, and was thirty-two—rather a great age to begin his career as a public figure, compared with most of the musicians we have been thinking about.

From then onward his life was full of interesting events. He became mixed up in politics—he wanted to put the whole world right as well as the musical profession—and lived in exile in Switzerland for eight years for making a dangerous political speech. During this period, however, he was busy composing. When he was forty-six he went to Paris again, and this time he managed to get the opera-house to stage *Tannhäuser*. But the audience behaved so badly at the performance that it could not be finished. Nearly three years later Wagner was given permission to return to Germany, but his first few years there were fraught with difficulties—financial and otherwise. Then, however, he was saved by a new admirer: the eighteen-year-old King Ludwig II of Bavaria. The King sent him a message: "Come here and finish your work." Now at last Wagner was able to work in peace at his huge operas, free from worry about money, and free from the hard routine of opera-directing. He did not 'live happily ever after'—far from it—but from this time onward he seemed able to make all his musical dreams come true.

What were these dreams? They were nothing less than a completely new idea of the whole purpose of music in the world. He was never *quite* sure, admittedly, what this idea was, but, from what we read, it seems that it was based on the following theories:

1. Music on its own was a dull business. It only really came to life when linked with words and action.

2. Music, plus poetry, plus acting, plus scenery, and the whole machinery of the theatre stage, all working together in *his* operas, was going to be the highest form of art of the future.

Did he succeed in carrying his idea out? He certainly did, as far as any human being could. Only two weaknesses began to show as his work went on. The first was the fact that his music was much better than his poetry; the second was that he could not prevent himself from explaining everything that was going on in his operas.

His great characters (King Mark in *Tristan*, Wotan in *The Ring*, Hans Sachs in *The Mastersingers* are all liable to embark on long speeches; they become school-masters and lecture the audience on the subject of the opera, instead of allowing them to form their own ideas. This holding-forth is done to very beautiful music, but the music does not always prevent yawns.

Most of the stories he tells in his operas are legends, and the characters in them are more than characters—they are ideas. They are more than life-size. Wagner makes sure of this by giving his characters and the ideas they stand for tunes of their own—'leading motifs' (p. 129). Whenever these characters appear, or are talked about, we hear their 'signature-tune' in the orchestra; this causes them to become ideas—heroism, evil, chivalry, love, atonement. So that at the end of a Wagner opera we seem to have heard a whole story of ideas and moods told by the orchestra, but made all the more real to us because we have had in front of our eyes the people who stand for those ideas.

How complicated opera has come to be! Gone are the simple days when Handel, Mozart, or Rossini could tell their operatic stories in songs, trios, quartets, and choruses. In Wagner the singers talk to each other in long, long lines of melody; only occasionally do they sing together, and they never sing a song unless the story tells them to, as it does in *Tannhäuser* and *The Mastersingers*, where they compete with each other for a prize given for the best performance of a song. And always there is the orchestra, pouring out rivers of sound, binding the stories together, and helping the characters to express their moods and thoughts.

Wagner's way of writing music was certainly 'the music of the future.' Nearly all composers at the beginning of this century found themselves writing like Wagner, especially if they were writing music for the orchestra. But, not being Wagner, they were not often very good at it. Perhaps the best opera written by another composer in the style of Wagner that we can still hear to-day in *Hansel and Gretel*, by Engelbert Humperdinck. This has all the best points of Wagner's style in it, and none of the weaker ones, such as the speechifying and the monotonous poetry.

But when we hear the 'Ride of the Valkyries,' the 'Pilgrims' Chorus,' the sea-music in *The Flying Dutchman*, or the overture to *The Mastersingers* we become caught up in the sheer loveliness and excitement of the sound of the orchestra as Wagner used it. We are quite content to forget his long-winded theories and speeches.

His operas were such a new experience for the singers of his day that they had to learn a new way of singing; conductors had to learn new ways too—and Wagner taught them all. He soon found, too, that the usual kind of theatre was in many ways unsuitable for his new operas, so he raised money and built a special one! He chose a little town called Bayreuth, which is a country town like Barnard Castle or Burford, and here, on the side of a hill, he built his 'Festival Theatre.' It was planned so that every one could get an equally good view of the stage; nearly every row had a door at the side of it, so that people did not have to push their way down centre-gangways; most important, the orchestra was sunk well below the stage and closed in from the audience's side, and so, of course, was the conductor. There was nothing to distract the audience's attention from the mighty happenings on the stage and from the music.

Here, in 1876, Wagner's dreams of opera indeed came true. The Bayreuth theatre was opened with the first complete performance of *The Ring*, the mightiest opera in the world, sung and played by great musicians who had come under Wagner's spell, and who had thrown up their other work in order to learn this strange new music. Later came Wagner's last opera, *Parsifal*, a story of the Knights of the Holy Grail, which Wagner wrote especially for his theatre, and which at first he forbade other opera-houses to perform. It must be performed only at

Bayreuth, and audiences must come there as pilgrims to hear it. Bayreuth became a shrine, and will be linked with Wagner for as long as Stratford-on-Avon is linked with Shakespeare. Here, to this day, we can see and hear this great man's life's-work in his own theatre: we can experience the famous 'Bayreuth hush' as the lights go down, and from the hidden orchestra comes the sound of the gradual welling-up of the River Rhine; we can see Brünnhilde ride her horse into the flames of the funeral-pyre, and the destruction by fire of Valhalla, the home of the ancient German gods.

If you asked an opera-lover to whistle one of Wagner's tunes for you he might not be able to oblige. He would certainly whistle a 'leading motif' (the 'Sword' theme, perhaps, or the Pilgrims' Chorus), but he would find it hard to put it across to you. But ask him to whistle a tune from Verdi's operas, and he would not be able to stop. You would probably get the whole of the 'Miserere' scene from *Il Trovatore*, the famous tune from *Rigoletto* (which was kept as a 'top-secret' until the first night of the opera), and great chunks of *La Traviata*, followed by *Aïda*.

Giuseppe Verdi, born in the same year as Wagner, was for most of his long life a 'normal' opera-composer. That is to say, he was not concerned about 'the music of the future,' and he had no desire to preach or teach on the operatic stage. What he did was to take strong, dramatic stories, with vivid characters in them, and set them to music which would enable the singers to sing their hearts out in solos, quartets, choruses, etc. They were 'singers' operas.' and seem to have been inspired by the famous saying of Rossini that "in opera, there is only one thing— voice, more voice, and still more voice." While Wagner, then, was using the operatic stage to put forth theories Verdi was giving operatic singers the kind of music they were used to, and which they loved to sing. For half their lives Verdi and Wagner remained ignorant of each other's work; one lived in Italy and the other mainly in Germany. Neither took any notice of the other. It was only later that Verdi, like every one else, found himself thinking about music in Wagner's manner.

Verdi lived until 1901; with him we arrive at last in our own century. Several stories are told about his young days which make it seem remarkable that he lived at all to write his music. When he was twelve months old his village was suddenly filled with foreign troops on their way through Italy, who began to break into houses and rob and loot. The women, including Verdi's mother with the little boy in her arms, took refuge in the church. But the troops broke down the door, and killed and wounded them. Mrs Verdi had the presence of mind to climb into the belfry and hide there behind a pile of timber until the soldiers had gone. Ten years later the boy, now organist of a little church some miles away, lost his way in the dark, and fell into a deep and icy canal. Luckily some one happened to be passing and fished him out—just in time.

He was nearly seven before his parents and teachers realized that he was full of music, and this was also brought home to them through an accident! The young Verdi was acting as server in Mass one day at the local church. When the organ started the boy became so lost in wonder at the sound of the music that he forgot about his duties as server, which enraged the priest so much that he gave him a kick that sent him tumbling to the foot of the steps, where he knocked his head on the floor and stunned himself. Afterwards he was sent for lessons to the very organist whose music had enthralled him.

The rest of his life is a chronicle of his operas, and we need not bother about it. What is important is his place in our musical picture, especially in relation to the other great force in opera—Wagner. We can compare them like this:

Wagner's singers sang 'endless melodies,' just as if they were speaking in song. Verdi's singers sang tunes, which could be quite easily taken out of the operas and sung by themselves.

Wagner's orchestra was all-important. If you took it away and left the singers to themselves the music would be reduced to nonsense. Verdi's orchestra was always just an accompaniment, though a very rich and beautiful one. If it were suddenly to stop during a performance, leaving the singers on their own, the opera would still make some kind of sense.

Wagner made all his characters into ideas. Verdi made them into people—slightly more than life-size, perhaps and very dramatic, but always human.

Wagner wrote all his own words. Verdi relied on words supplied by other men, and in his old age was fortunate to secure the services of a very able writer, Arrigo Boito, with whom he could work happily and confidently.

Wagner made his operas out of most complicated webs of sound. There were the 'leading motifs,' the sound-effects, and the picture-music (such as that which accompanies the burning-down of Valhalla)—all making up a sort of running commentary on the story of the opera, and all played by the large orchestra. But Verdi was often quite content to let the orchestra play, "oom-pa-pa," while the singers expressed everything they felt, and told the whole story, in full-throated song.

After writing one opera after another, frankly for money, Verdi had a rest for nearly sixteen years. During that time Wagner's operas began to be played every-where, and Verdi must have heard some of them. After Wagner died in 1883 Verdi was the only great operatic composer still living, and he astonished the musical world by bringing out two operas which showed that he had taken a great deal of notice of Wagner's work. These were *Otello*, written when he was seventy-four, and *Falstaff*, written when he was eighty. The words of both these operas were supplied by Boito, and were based on Shakespeare's *Othello* and *The Merry Wives of Windsor*. His audiences did not like these operas very much, but we realize now that even Verdi, with all his love of music which would appeal to the masses, was looking forward into the future alongside his great German partner, Richard Wagner.

10

Music speaks with an Accent

IN Chopin's Polonaises and Mazurkas we can hear the people of Poland singing and dancing. From the middle of the 1800's there were sounds reaching us from many other countries. On the map of Europe lights began to glow not only in Germany and Italy, but in several dark patches, stretching from the Mediterranean to the Arctic Circle. Music began to have a dialect; it was becoming a part of *nations*, like their customs, their food, and their weather.

Russia

Though Russia and music go quite easily together in our minds we are inclined to think of Russia's music either as sung in churches by choirs with enormously deep bass voices, or as played in places of entertainment by small, energetic orchestras. On one side are the devout chantings, and on the other the heart-rending folk-songs and the feverish Cossack dances. Music of these two kinds, religious and popular, had been going on in all countries, of course, but we know Russia's better than that of most countries because, quite simply, it is so good, and so appealing to our ears.

It was some time, however, before Russian music found its way into the concert-hall and the opera-house. The large country houses had their private orchestras and singers, as they had in Germany and Austria; but they played and sang Italian music. The books the Russians read, and the plays they saw in the theatres, were French, German, or English. At the beginning of the 1800's, with all the changes in mood that the Romantic era brought, the time was ripe for Russian writers and musicians to make their art speak for their own country, to sing their own people's praises in poetry, and to write music which, wherever it was heard, would make the listeners say, "That must be Russian music."

In about 1830 a young man called Michael Glinka had to leave his job in Moscow and go to Italy because of his bad health. He had always been full of music, and he lost no time in making his way to operas and concerts during his travels in Italy. He resolved to write operas. He travelled home via Germany (where he had some lessons in composition) and read the poems and stories of the great Russian writer, Pushkin, who was at that time putting Russia's history into strong, vigorous poetry. With *A Life for the Tsar* and *Russlan and Ludmilla* Glinka showed how Russian tunes and rhythms could be brought into the opera-house from the cafés and the open air. But for us Glinka is not much more than a pioneer; he is a 'Signpost Chapter' musician. We do not hear his music very often now; only his overture to *Russlan and Ludmilla* is regularly heard (it is a very tuneful and attractive one too).

There were soon other names to follow. A group of composers arose whose music is among the most popular in the world; nearly all of it was written between 1860 and 1900. Modeste Mussorgsky, an army officer, gave us music that is rough, violent, and brutal; his opera *Boris Godunov*, his orchestral piece *A Night on the Bare Mountain*, and his group of piano pieces called *Pictures from an Exhibition* bring us in touch with a powerful personality. Mussorgsky seems to be a kind of giant—immensely strong, rugged, and apparently primitive, but inspired, and suddenly roaring forth beautiful poetry in a strong dialect.

Alexander Borodin, a professor of chemistry, wrote music which gave off lovely sound as a rose gives off its distinctive scent; in his string quartets and his opera *Prince Igor* there are such beautiful tunes that musicians in the rest of Europe poured scorn on them for quite a long time—they were thought too tuneful to be *really* good!

Nicholas Rimsky-Korsakov was an officer in the Russian Imperial Navy, who wrote his first symphony on board ship during the Navy's winter cruise. When it was played at a concert in St Petersburg the audience was highly delighted to see a young man in naval uniform come on to receive the applause. There was only an old harmonium on board his ship, "but," said Rimsky-Korsakov, "we spent some considerable time ashore in Gravesend, where there was a public house which had a good piano. I used to try my symphony out on it." One wonders what the customers must have thought, and whether the public house with the good piano still exists in Gravesend!

Rimsky-Korsakov was a master of the orchestra. He spent a good deal of his life experimenting in the sounds that an orchestra could make, and one has only to listen to *Scheherezade*, a suite based on four stories from the *Arabian Nights*, to hear what brilliant and exciting effects he could conjure from orchestral players.

And finally there was Peter Tchaikovsky, the most popular of all the nineteenth-century Russian composers —and the least Russian! He was first a civil servant, until music was too strong for him. He differed in several ways from the other composers we have been discussing. He did not make such an important thing of national music as they did, and did not join their circle. He did not use many folk-tunes to make his music sound Russian, though there is no mistaking its Russian flavour. He felt that music should be international—that is to say, that it should be written so that it could be enjoyed by people of all countries, and not just by the fellow-countrymen of the composer. He did not write music based on Russian legends or history (except for an opera or two) but used the usual musical shapes: symphonies, concertos, sonatas, quartets. His music has more heart than the other composers' music—and the heart is on its sleeve! When

Tchaikovsky is feeling happy or miserable there is no doubt about it. His beautiful tunes and his great thundering climaxes of sound are the composer himself, singing his heart out. It is just as if a very excitable person were to stand at a street corner and tell the passers-by all about his joys and troubles—his private difficulties, his family affairs, and his dreams. Some listeners are embarrassed to have to listen to such intimate talk; others find it first-rate entertainment. When one hears the huge opening battery of piano chords in the Piano Concerto in B flat minor, with the bravest tune in the world thundering out on the orchestra, one feels at once that life is a magnificent business; but when the last movement of the 'Pathetic' symphony sobs and moans to its close there seems to be no hope left. . . . At the next minute, with the ballet music (*Swan Lake* and the *Nutcracker Suite*), we are taken into an enchanted land where joys and sorrows are no longer human ones, but those of fairyland.

Perhaps you have noticed that all these Russian composers started life doing something other than music. Only Tchaikovsky and Rimsky-Korsakov became fully-fledged musicians, and even they chose other careers in their early days, as we have seen. Some of the composers (including Rimsky-Korsakov, but not Tchaikovsky) seemed to work in a kind of co-operative society. For instance, Borodin's *Prince Igor* (which he left unfinished at his death) was completed by Rimsky-Korsakov and a younger composer, Alexander Glazounov; Mussorgsky's *Boris Godunov* had its orchestral part completely re-written by Rimsky-Korsakov—and so on. Between them, these men made Russian music shine with a bright light.

Bohemia (*Czechoslovakia*)

This attractive country, with its exciting history, has given the rest of the world one kind of music which every one knows and loves. It is a dance—the Polka. The "one-two-three-hop!" rhythm of the Polka swept across Europe in the nineteenth century. Our staid ancestors in Queen Victoria's reign flung themselves round the ballrooms to it, losing ribbons and hairpins, and shouting,

> Ha, ha, ha, you and me,
> Little brown jug, don't I love thee.

It is not surprising, then, that such a vigorous rhythm should have beaten strongly in the heads of Czechoslovakia's composers. There are many of them, but we need only mention two: Smetana and Dvořák. Both these great composers wrote their music in the middle and late 1800's.

Bedřich Smetana was the first composer to teach us to enjoy the native musical language of Czechoslovakia; he was also the first to prove to his own countrymen that they had some beautiful music to give to the world. He was a fervent patriot. His greatest work was a set of six symphonic poems, called *My Fatherland*, in which he describes his country in all its moods. The best known is *Vltava*, which describes in a long, glorious tune the course of the great Czech river after which it is named. His comic opera, *The Bartered Bride*, sparkles with all the vitality and humour of the country's peasants, and beneath the story lies a patriotic message of encouragement to the people of Bohemia, who were under foreign rule at the time the opera was produced. Like Beethoven, Smetana became deaf towards the end of his life, but before that the disease showed itself in a continuous high-pitched note which ran in his head while he was composing. It must have been distracting in the extreme; in fact, the long note does appear in two of his last works, especially the String Quartet.

Smetana is less well-known to us than his great fellow-countryman Antonin Dvořák. Dvořák was yet another composer whose music seemed to gush out in endless *tune*. Like Schubert, he could think of a wisp of melody, and—hey presto—off he went straight to the end of a large symphony without taking a breath!

He started life very modestly—as a butcher's boy.

When he was sixteen he began to study music seriously, and paid for his lessons by playing in cafés. At that time he knew hardly anything about the great composers who had gone before; "Beethoven and Mozart were just names to me," he wrote. After about ten years as an orchestral player he began to attract notice with his music. Brahms saw some of it, and recommended him to a publisher; and Dvořák soon made money both for himself and his publisher by producing the popular *Slavonic Dances*. These were soon played as piano duets all over Europe, and are still as popular as ever. He followed these up with choral works, which were just right for the big festivals which so delighted musicians in this country in Victorian times, and he was a thrice-welcome visitor to Leeds, Birmingham and the other festival centres.

He went to the U.S.A. for three years to direct the National Conservatory (school of music) in New York, and while he was there he found himself thinking of tunes which had a decidedly 'negro-spiritual' twist. His best-known symphony, the 'New World,' is full of them, and so is his String Quartet in F, sometimes called 'The Nigger.'

Dvořák was Czechoslovakia's musical ambassador. Like Tchaikovsky in Russia, he was able to speak his country's musical language with an 'educated' accent, so that people in other countries could understand it. There was always a danger that national music would belong so firmly to its own country that other people would find it unattractive, just as some people cannot eat Indian curry, or macaroni, or garlic. As we shall see later, this happened to English music at the beginning of this century. But Bohemian music spread rapidly and easily over Europe; it lit up concert-halls and opera-houses which were often in danger of being shrouded in a kind of deep purple mist of German Romanticism.

France

We left the French musical world trying to settle itself

after the Revolution. Berlioz was thundering his music at them; Wagner was quietly told to go home; Chopin was charming them with his pale countenance and his piano-playing; Liszt was dazzling them. What of the other composers? Was anyone, in fact, speaking music with a French accent among these foreign visitors who were crowding Paris musical life?

It was not until the second half of the 1800's that France began to speak its own language in music. Before that music in France meant opera, and the French opera was 'entertainment music' rather than music that audiences could live on, as they live on bread and butter! Charles Gounod produced his opera *Faust,* built on the favourite Romantic story of the selling of a man's soul to the devil in return for a favour. This is still a great favourite; at the first performance the 'Soldiers' Chorus' nearly 'stopped the show.' But *Faust* would never mean 'France' to any listener. Georges Bizet wrote an opera which is now the most popular in the world, but it is a story of Spain, and is called *Carmen.* The music is so tied up with the Spanish element in the story that to some people it comes as quite a surprise to learn that the composer was a Frenchman. Then there were the delicious operettas (musical comedies) which the French audiences loved, and which will find their way into the chapter on light music.

French music, then, was largely stage music—light and tuneful, but not nourishing; it was strawberries and cream rather than roast beef and Yorkshire pudding.

One composer alone kept his head amid all the excitement of brilliant piano-playing, noisy orchestras, and sparkling operettas. This was an organist called César Franck. He was a Belgian by birth, but he lived in Paris nearly all his life, and was organist at a famous city church. Hardly anyone knew him as a composer. To the musicians of Paris he was either a brilliant organist who could improvise beautiful music, or a gentle but inspiring teacher. In fact no one would have thought it possible that he could have written such sparkling music as the *Symphonic Variations* for piano and orchestra or the Violin Sonata. He has not left us much music, but it is all evergreen in the affections of musicians. Every orchestra plays the symphony; every group of chamber-music players knows the String Quartet, the Piano Quintet, and the Violin Sonata; every Pianist has played the Symphonic Variations and the Prelude, Chorale, and Fugue; and every organist knows and loves the music he has written for that instrument. César Franck brought the 'roast beef' back into French music at a time when audiences were feeding on either frothy confections (light operas) or soggy cake that had failed to rise (Romantic dramas).

At the same time a slightly younger man was realizing that France must put itself more firmly on the serious musical map. This was Camille Saint-Saëns. He wrote a tremendous amount of music, and he was driven by a burning desire to show the musical world that what the Germans could do the French could do better. He wrote symphonic poems in the style of Liszt, chamber music which sounds like Mendelssohn, piano music which is a mixture of Liszt and Schumann, and a famous opera, *Samson and Delilah*, which is like a Mendelssohn oratorio. Some one once said that he was "the greatest composer in the world who wasn't a genius." Nevertheless, he helped the cause of French music enormously during his long life (he lived to be eighty-six), and among his works there are many pieces of music we would not care to be without. One of his most popular and lovable works is the *Animals' Carnival*, for two pianos and orchestra; here we have *The March of the Lions, The Donkey. The Aquarium, The Cuckoo*, and—yes—even *Human Beings Practising the Piano!* To Saint-Saëns anything that breathed was an 'Animal.' The most famous of the 'Zoo' is *The Swan*, a lovely tune for cello, to which the great dancer Pavlova danced an immortal dance. Saint-Saëns could write a good tune, and he could give every instrument and every voice under the sun a grateful and exciting kind of music to play or sing. Like Tchaikovsky in Russia, and Dvořák in Bohemia, he was able to write national music which 'exported' easily to other countries. It is neat, elegant, civilized, melodious—but one never feels that he *had* to write any of it.

Saint-Saëns, like Franck, did a lot of teaching, and it was through his pupils rather than through his own music that he helped to make French music live its own life. Chief among these was Gabriel Fauré. Listening to Fauré's music is like standing in the formally laid-out garden of a French château. The flowers are white, mauve, and crimson. At noon they blaze with colour; at dusk they are a luminous glow, but the formal patterns of the flowerbeds can still be seen. It is difficult to describe this mixture of colour, shadow, and pattern that makes Fauré's music so attractive. It is a perfect blending of the *sound* and the *shape* of music. And sometimes, as in the *Pavane* for orchestra or the Requiem for chorus and orchestra, there is an *ancient* sound about the music, as if it had been thought of a thousand years ago. For the first time France had found a truly native composer, to express (in the music of the nineteenth century) her neatness, her shapely, veiled beauty, and her ageless depth of feeling. Fauré is a 'musician's composer'; he has not written any music which has become world-famous, like Tchaikovsky's ballet music, or Chopin's piano music. Many pianists have yet to discover his Nocturnes, Barcarolles, and Preludes; many singers have not yet realized that his songs are among the finest since those of Schubert. His music is never showy; there are no loud noises to be made in it. Like Schumann, he speaks to us affectionately, at close quarters; he does not storm at us from the concert-platform.

If, however, you were to ask the average musical listener to name one French composer he would almost certainly say, "Debussy." He would know the piano pieces *Clair de Lune*, and *The Golliwog's Cake-walk*, and the orchestral tone-poem *L'Après-midi d'un Faune*; and he would have in his mind a vague impression of 'misty' musical sound, the kind you get from a piano if you play it with the right-hand (sustaining) pedal firmly pressed down. He would be quite right, for it is this sort of musical sound that Claude Achille Debussy explored. He was not anxious to put down clear-cut musical thoughts in clear-cut sound, as Mozart or Beethoven did; nor did he wish to tell a romantic story in great splurges of orchestral noise as Liszt or Berlioz did. He always tried to get farther than the thought, the story, or the picture, and to give an *impression* of them in sound. Now, it is not easy to see the difference between that process and the Romantic one. Let us see if we can show it in words. Here are three ways of describing the same thing:

The *Classical* way (Mozart, Beethoven, etc.):

The train—gleaming, rejoicing in its power—roared into the station. With mingled hope and despair we prospective travellers sought for places amid the crush of folk already aboard. We were received with compassion, and proceeded on our journey.

The *Romantic* way (Berlioz, Liszt, etc.):

Great Heavens! The train at last approached! Like some fiery monster from Hades itself, here it came, belching forth darksome billows of evil smoke, emitting flames of daemonic fire. Thousands of human souls which were aboard sat in attitudes of frozen immobility, awaiting, as it were, their final destruction. At last the fearsome apparition came to rest, and at that moment, as if at a signal, the hordes of clamorous beings around me surged madly towards the monster's gaping mouths, bearing me blindly with them. Ah, ye Gods, would I too be swallowed up and borne to the Land of Shadows?

The *Impressionistic* way (Debussy):

Louder, louder, louder! Hiss of steam, gleaming steely bulk; fires aglow towards the darkling sky; slowing, slowing, s-l-o-w-i-n-g—STOP! People rushing, pushing; blind, surging crowd; hot, weary, urgent, laden. Slam, slam, slam, whistle, forward-moving, slowly, faster, faster! . . .

Thus a simple scene can be described either as a straightforward story, or as the product of a highly-coloured imagination, or an *impression,* using words merely to sketch in the impressions we have when we wait for a crowded long-distance train. It was in this way that Debussy used musical sound. When he wanted to suggest 'Mists,' or 'The Wind on the Plain,' or 'Fire-works,' as he did in his Preludes for the piano, he wrote *wisps* of melody, or continuous rushing passages of rapid notes, or bright, sudden splashes. The right-hand pedal became very important; it had to be used a great deal to blur the edges of the tunes, and to run handfuls of rapid notes into one *wash* of sound. Debussy also made good use of a scale (known as the *whole-tone scale*) in which all the notes are the same distance apart, like this:

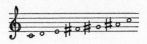

If you play these notes softly on the piano, keeping the right-hand pedal pressed down all the time, you will pro-duce the kind of sound that Debussy used very often to give us his impressions of a scene or a story. Listen some time to his Prelude called *The Cathedral under the Water.* He suggests the very vivid French story of a cathedral at the bottom of a lake, which rises to the sur-face one night; the lights are burning, the choir is singing, the organ is playing, and a large bell is tolling. Debussy conjures up the scene beautifully in piano sound. It is especially vivid at the moment when the cathedral begins to sink back into the depths of the water. The singing, the organ, the bell, and even the outlines of the cathedral itself can be *heard* to become gradually blurred and shifting as the water closes over.

Debussy's name is often linked with that of another French composer, Maurice Ravel. One can see why when one hears Ravel's piano pieces, especially *Jeux d'Eau* (*Fountains*) or his music for the ballet *Daphnis and Chloe*. Ravel was thirteen years younger than Debussy (he was born in 1875, and belongs to the 1900's rather than to the last century), and his music gradually moved away from the veiled, splashy sounds of impressionism. It became neater, with sharp edges to its tunes; it contained fewer notes, but each one was important to the mood of the piece. He tried several musical experiments, and they all succeeded. The most famous one is the *Bolero*, which he wrote for a famous dancer to dance to. Ravel wanted some music that got louder and more exciting right from beginning to end, but without getting faster. So he wrote a long tune and repeated it over and over again, against a background of the bolero rhythm played on a side-drum. As the piece goes on the tune and the rhythm are hammered relentlessly into our ears until they become almost unbearable; and just when we feel we cannot stand any more it suddenly comes to an end. The timing of it is perfect: all the while we can hear the tune played on more and more instruments until the whole orchestra is hard at work.

Ravel brings us right up to the Second World War—he died in 1937—and since then no French composer has shown real greatness. A Frenchman said recently that "France has not produced any giants in music." With the possible exception of Berlioz, he may be right. The musical world prefers to listen to music which has got *weight*, like that of Bach and Beethoven. So strong is the influence of the great German masters that even in these days we are inclined to distrust the value of music which merely 'sounds nice.' French music is regarded as the dessert course in the musical meal, to follow the good, solid fare of the main course. In fact this applies to most national music; even to-day it almost seems that only German music can be understood all the world over, from Lapland to Timbuctoo, from Edinburgh to Buenos Aires; music by composers of other lands is 'slipped into the programme' to give colour and light relief.

Norway and Sweden

It is very easy to identify the music of Norway and Sweden. Their songs and dances have a very strong local accent. Both countries have produced a good many composers, but the one we know best is the Norwegian, Edvard Grieg. "The gentle Grieg" was born in Bergen, and was very insistent on being thought of as Norwegian, not just 'Scandinavian.' Like most of the successful national composers, he soaked himself in the folk-music and dances of his country and went to Germany to learn how to write it all down. He has left us a great number of charming *Lyric Pieces* for the piano; among them are pieces with such names as *The Butterfly*, *To the Spring*, and *The Dance of the Gnomes*, and they all speak with the unmistakable voice of Grieg. Now and then he could roar like a lion, as he does in his Piano Concerto, which he wrote when he was twenty-five. In this he speaks to us through a megaphone—the piano storms and rants, and the orchestra aids and abets it. There are most beautiful tunes, which seem to have come straight from the Norwegian mountain-tops, and there are rousing dances from the town-square. But when all the noise has died down we find ourselves turning back to the *Lyric Pieces*, the songs—the *small* music—to find the real Grieg speaking to us in music about Norway.

Finland

It seems strange that our musical history has taken us right from the sunny skies of Italy and the mild, fog-bound climate of England, where music flourished in the early days, to a country right in the Arctic Circle, with a latitude of 65 degress. Yet here, in Finland, came music from a composer who, besides writing the national music of his country, did a great deal to change the face of orchestral music. Though he died at a great age in 1957, and was apparently composing almost to the end, he allowed us to hear hardly any new works after 1925. His name was Jan Sibelius.

Sibelius wrote symphonic poems, lots of small pieces and songs, a violin concerto, a string quartet, and eight symphonies. (We have not yet heard the eighth, which he forbade to be played until after his death.) In these works he did three important things:

1. He expressed the folk-lore of Finland in music by turning many of Finland's legends into music, in the form of symphonic poems. (The Finnish Government allowed him a pension for many years, and made his birthday a national holiday. This had never happened before to a composer.)

2. At a time when composers in other countries were seeing how much noise they could make, and how much colour and excitement they could get into their music, Sibelius went back to the orchestra that had served Beethoven and Brahms so well, and wrote music for it that caused the listener to *think* as well as to *feel*. He once said that whereas other modern composers offered the public cocktails of every description, he simply offered them pure cold water.

3. He tried out a new way of writing symphonies. He found himself moving away from the old pattern of a symphonic movement (p. 96) in which a composer (*a*) gives us his two main ideas (first and second subject) complete, (*b*) proceeds to break them up, discuss them, and develop them, and (*c*) puts them together again. Sibelius lets us see him at work in his workshop. We see him making scraps of melody and rhythm, putting them together, arranging them in different shapes, and *finally* turning to present us with the finished article. In his later symphonies, the Sixth and Seventh, he does this so brilliantly that we feel we are present at the creation of a new

world. There is a smoky chaos of sound; into it are hurled jagged little fragments of tune; they swirl and toss in the gloom; gradually they grow in power; our ears connect them up and link them together. At last, just when we know we are waiting for it, the main idea of the symphony thunders out at us—fully grown, complete, and magnificent.

Sibelius is a giant in music, and not only on account of the new aspects of music which he has shown us. His music has a very strong and distinctive flavour. Much of it is dark in tone and atmosphere (he is fond of dark-sounding instruments, such as the cor anglais and the viola), but he uses *darkness* of sound to create beautiful and haunting music. His tone-poem *The Swan of Tuonela* should be heard as an example of his musical language. The very name sounds dark, desolate, and mysterious. Tuonela is the underworld of Finland's legends; to get there the soul has to voyage over nine seas, until it comes to the last barrier: a river encircling Tuonela, on which floats the Sacred Swan. Now, you can't make music sound like a swan, or a river, or an island. Music will just seem to sound like those things if you tell people first. But what you *can* do is to think of a swan, swimming on a river encircling an island of the dead, and there you have an atmosphere, a darkling remote mood, which can be translated into musical sounds. This Sibelius does, in only about a hundred bars of music, but with such haunting expressiveness that we seem to be brought to the dark shadowland on the edge of the world where, to the sound of the shimmering strings and the desolate tone of the cor anglais, we see the fateful Swan—"the long-necked, graceful swimmer, swimming in the black death-river, in the sacred stream. . . ."

Russia, Czechoslovakia, France, Norway, Finland—musical lights were glowing all over the map of Europe at the beginning of the 1900's. Nor were these all. In

Hungary, a country which has been mentioned more than once in this story of music (Schubert worked there, Liszt captured its folk-music in his piano Rhapsodies, Brahms knew it well) some important music was being written. Erno von Dohnányi wrote music which speaks Hungarian to us with a German accent—that of Brahms; Zoltán Kodály (still living) has given us orchestral and church music as seen through the eyes of the fierce gipsies who come from that country. But the country's musical giant is Béla Bartók. Bartók, who died in 1945, is still thought of by many present-day music-lovers as the man who "brought wrong notes into music!" To many people the name 'Bartók' means 'nasty noise.' But, in these space-ship days, try to imagine Hungary as a planet in the Universe on which very clever people live. Suddenly, in a flying saucer, or whatever transport between the planets happened to be popular at the time, there arrives a brilliant musician who has lots of most important things to say to us through his music. He causes orchestras, string quartets, and pianists to make the most extraordinary noises, but somehow we listeners say to ourselves, We can't understand his language; it sounds perfectly horrible to us, like a thousand goods-trains shunting in the middle of the night. But we can't stop listening, because he is trying to tell us something very important —something we must know. So we *must* try to learn this visitor's language. We must hear him again and again, just as we listened to our parents while we were trying to learn English as babies! That is how the intelligent listener regards the music of Bartók: he can't help feeling that Bartók is telling him something important, no matter how unfamiliar the sound of his telling it may be.

From Spain too there came some attractive music. The ballet-suites of Manuel de Falla (*The Three-cornered Hat* and *Love the Magician*) and the piano music of Enrique Granados and Isaac Albéniz enabled us to hear the national voice of Spain in the theatre and the concert-hall. Granados has given us a delightful series of piano pieces based on the paintings and tapestries of the Spanish painter Goya; he also wrote an opera based on these pieces, and went to New York to see it performed. On the way back (in 1916) he and his wife were drowned at sea when his ship was torpedoed by a German submarine. Albéniz began life as a pianist; this is almost literally true, as he gave his first recital when he was four. He must have been a wonderfully adventurous boy; when he was nine he stowed away on a ship to South America, and gave piano recitals (which he organized himself) all over Mexico and the South of U.S.A. He was completely independent; he made and lost money without worrying about it, and life seemed to treat him well. Later he gave up playing and turned to composition. In a set of very difficult piano pieces he makes Spain live for us in music. He 'dressed up' Spanish popular tunes and dances in most complicated garb; a pianist seems to need more fingers than he has been born with. But the results are most attractive to listen to and very great fun to play.

England and the United States of America—where do these two great countries stand in our history? In serious music the U.S.A. has not yet given us much to think about. There is time yet. Music, like an oak-tree, takes a long time to grow, and perhaps the seeds are being safely planted by such composers as Samuel Barber, Gian-Carlo Menotti, and Aaron Copland, all of whom are writing music that is meaning something to the rest of the world. But it is in its new folk-music (which people call jazz) that the U.S.A. speaks to us in its national voice, and which we will consider later in this book. As for England, it is soon to have a chapter to itself.

Modern Trends: Schönberg and Stravinsky

SIGNPOSTS usually point two ways: the way we have come and the way we are going. At this stage in history (we are now at about 1912) this is certainly the case.

We left Wagner in Chapter 9, looking as far ahead as any musician has ever done. Hosts of people copied his way of writing opera, and his way of dealing with large orchestras. They wrote 'endless melody' for their opera-singers instead of set songs, and noble, sweeping orchestral music in which enormous bodies of players were needed. Among these composers were Richard Strauss, who, as late as 1948, was still writing songs which could almost have been written by Wagner. Gustav Mahler and Anton Bruckner each wrote nine enormous symphonies, using Wagner's orchestra. All these men looked back in their music. It seemed not to matter to them that music was marching forward around them—past them. They marked the end of a historical chapter.

While Richard Strauss was writing his luscious operas a young Austrian composer near by, called Arnold Schönberg, was looking into the future. He had already written music just like Wagner's, but bigger, louder, and poorer. Then he suddenly became sated with big noises and orchestras, and began to express himself in a most economical and quiet manner. The sounds he wrote were completely unintelligible at first (at a London concert he was once hissed by the audience) until musicians began to realize that he was using some different kind of musical language. Briefly, the difference is this:

When we listen to music we 'understand' we can

follow it because it keeps to a sort of alphabet of eight main notes, which we call a scale. These eight notes are the most important ones, and any others in the music sound like decorations; they seem to be there just to give *colour* to the music, like this:

But Schönberg said to himself, Why should any notes be more important than the others? Let's make them all equal, then we'll be able to make up much richer tunes, because instead of having only eight main notes we'll have twelve:

Now let us think what the same sort of difference would be in terms of language. Using the eight notes of our ordinary scale, we can make up a tune which makes just as much sense as the sentence, "The cat sat on the mat." If, however, we use the 'colour-notes' in between we can add colour to our sentence: "The *ginger* cat sat *lazily* on the *hairy, black, and yellow* mat." It still makes perfect sense because we realize that "cat," "sat," and "mat" are the words which *really* matter. But to Schönberg they don't matter any more than the other words in the sentence. He, therefore, would feel quite justified in writing, "The ginger sat on black," or, "ginger cat the and yellow," or indeed he might alter the order of the words, and write, "mat yellow on lazily ginger," and so on. Musically, it means that Schönberg was not using a scale any more, but a *series* of notes. He kept to the same series throughout a piece of music, but he rearranged the notes of which it consisted in several different ways. This is difficult to understand, but it is so important that it must find its way into a book on musical development. For the *series* is being used more and more, and the *scale* less and less by modern composers throughout Europe. Just as, as we saw near the beginning of this book, the modes once gave way to the scales, it might be now that our old familiar scales are giving way to the *twelve-tone series* as a way of expressing music.

As we know by now, melody is only part of the musical picture. There is also rhythm. While Schönberg was experimenting with melody another composer was exploring rhythm. Igor Stravinsky, the Russian composer, was writing ballets for the famous Diaghilev Company: *The Firebird*, *Petrouchka*, and, most unusual of all, *The Rite of Spring*.

The Rite of Spring pushes complicated rhythm as far as it will go; it also needs a larger orchestra than ever. It is 'cave-man' music; it bludgeons the hearer into stunned submission by the sheer noise of the orchestra and the primitive juddering set up by the intricate weaving of all the various rhythms being played by each section of the orchestra. *The Rite of Spring* was obviously the end of another musical road. Neither Stravinsky himself nor anyone else could carry the same idea on any farther. Like Schönberg, he abandoned the idea of swollen, noisy music, and went to the other extreme. It was as if he were trying to discover how *few* players and notes he could use to obtain his musical effects. He aimed at getting his music to sound as clear as that of Mozart. In his latest opera, *The Rake's Progress*, he looks right back across the years to the eighteenth century; a whole world of music separates it from *The Rite of Spring*.

Schönberg left with us a new musical A B C. Stravinsky 'pepped up' the music of the beginning of this century with new and vital rhythms, and showed the way to simpler, clearer ways of writing music—ways that had been forgotten in the welter of noise that the Wagnerians were giving us.

11

English Music since 1700

IN Victorian times this country was called by the rest of Europe "the land without music." The last of our composers whose name meant anything to a German, an Italian, or a Frenchman was Handel—a visitor from Germany who became British because he liked working in England. Handel's music shone like a great white light over the English musical scene, and tended to dazzle people so that they did not notice some excellent British-born musicians who were working quietly in towns throughout the country.

There was John Stanley, the blind organist of the Temple Church in London, whose string concertos are quite beautiful, and speak to us with a softer and tenderer voice than Handel's. There was Charles Avison of Newcastle-on-Tyne, who alone was bold enough to say that Handel's music was not perfection itself, and who left us some charming music in the Italian style. A Warwickshire country vicar, Richard Mudge, was producing music in his candle-lit study which glows with warmth and throbs with power; it has been discovered and performed only during this last year.

Dr Thomas Arne, perhaps the greatest of them all, was a theatre musician who composed music to accompany plays at Drury Lane. His lovely songs from the Shakespeare plays (such as "Blow, blow, thou Winter Wind," "Where the Bee sucks," and "Under the Greenwood Tree") will always be among the best songs in the world. And there was William Boyce, composer to the Chapel Royal, whose anthems, birthday odes, and theatre-music are sunny, lightsome music, and were very popular in their day.

But still there were no giants. The 1700's did not produce a Mozart, nor the 1800's a Berlioz, a Liszt, or a Wagner. Those in this country who were writing music in the nineteenth century were content to imitate first Mendelssohn, and then Brahms. Their music was inartistic, dusty, and uninspired, and consisted mostly of tedious oratorios and cantatas to be performed at the huge choral festivals. If not quite "a land without music" England was certainly a land with third-rate music—until at last, almost at the end of the century, there were signs of change. Music now returned to England timidly, but unmistakably, and largely through the efforts of two composers, Parry and Stanford.

Sir Hubert Parry (Eton, Oxford, Royal College of Music) was a new kind of musician—a country gentleman, businessman, athlete, and administrator who is usually thought of as the first 'respectable' composer, writing his music in faultless morning dress and being always careful to appear 'normal' and English in the meantime. His music was considered typically English, too, which seemed to mean that he could write noble, elevated tunes like *Jerusalem*, or (indeed) *England*. This is the popular idea of Parry, but it is just not true. For all his bluff yachtsman's appearance and his hearty and efficient directing of the Royal College of Music he was a most sensitive, shy man; he was unhappy about his music, hated facing large crowds, and had very little confidence in himself. If one remembers that, and if one rids oneself of the feeling that Parry was an amateur musician who wrote too much music, one immediately finds new beauties in his songs and choral works, and one realizes that he stands head and shoulders above the pale German-copying English composers of the day. His great chorus *Blest Pair of Sirens*, a setting of Milton's words, is far, far more than a stodgy Doctor-of-Music exercise in eight-part counterpoint; it is a grand, sensitive, deeply-felt act of homage to Music and Verse which has never been surpassed either on this side of the Channel or the other. At the next moment we find him setting Browning's *Pied Piper of Hamelin*, with an elfin humour and a moving pathos that make us literally laugh at the Mayor of Hamelin and weep with the mothers of the children who were lured away.

Sir Charles Stanford (Cambridge, Royal College of Music) was an Irishman. He was a few years younger than Parry, and spent a long life teaching at the Royal College of Music while Parry was Director there. Like Parry, he wrote a vast amount of music—songs, symphonies, operas, choral works, church music. Perhaps he had a lighter touch than Parry, and a greater sense of humour. He certainly had a sense of *mystery* which seems to hark back to the work of Debussy. In his *Songs of the Fleet* he conjures up a haunting picture of the Fleet sailing at dawn; later in the same work he deals with the Admiral ("the little man whose voice you never hear"), who in a time of grave danger seemed to change into Nelson himself; and again he gives us the stillness and enchantment of the middle watch, when those on duty in the small hours feel themselves so very isolated and alone amid the huge surrounding sea. . . .

In Parry and Stanford, then, England found a 'Blest pair of Sirens' who gave us music with an English accent. This accent was still spoken with more than a touch of German in it (Stanford was a close friend of Brahms), but one was beginning to be able to say, "That is English music!"

Meanwhile a shy young man was growing up in the city of Worcester. He was the son of a local music-seller; soon he had taught himself to play several instruments, and had begun to write some music for local people to play. He never became Director of this or Principal of that, nor did he go to a University or a College of Music, and although he later became a 'Sir,' and also received the Order of Merit (the highest award in the country), he remained just himself—Elgar.

Edward Elgar was to be known as the first great

English composer since Purcell, who had finished his work in 1695. Here at last was an English musician who was held by even the Germans to be great. He became *our* composer—but not by writing music which contained folk-songs or dances round the maypole. Instead he appealed to our deep emotions. He expressed our love of country in the London overture *Cockaigne* and in the *Pomp and Circumstance* marches (one of which includes the tune which we know as "Land of Hope and Glory"); he interpreted the messages of the New Testament in a new way in his oratorios *The Apostles* and *The Kingdom*; he gave the Catholic view of the after-life in *The Dream of Gerontius*; and in his symphonies, concertos, and small orchestral pieces he showed us in music what a sensitive, impetuous, moody people we are, once we cease feeling that we must assert ourselves in the world. Elgar got straight to our inmost hearts.

Like Parry, Elgar loved to pass himself off as a country gentleman; he attended race-meetings, and hated it to be known by the outside world that he was a musician. It was still 'unEnglish' to be a full-time composer—but that is just what Elgar was. For the first time for nearly two hundred years we had a great composer who was a professional—who did his job with the same mastery with which we expect a cobbler or a plumber to do his. He wrote his rich, glowing music for large orchestras and choruses; he knew exactly how he wanted it to sound, and he gave every one difficult but very 'playable' parts to play. His noble tunes can always be recognized; in fact we call them "Elgarian" because they are so much a part of him. His music, like himself, is a strange mixture. Some of it is noisy and vulgar, and belongs to the hearty Edwardian times in which he lived; the rest (the Cello Concerto, the *Enigma Variations*, and the *Serenade for Strings*, for instance) is the work of an intensely sensitive and thoughtful man, whose emotions were very profoundly felt. In the slow movement of the First Symphony, in the closing pages of the Cello Concerto, and in the first movement of the Violin Concerto it is almost as if, like Schumann, he is telling us about himself in words, so clearly do his feelings show themselves in music.

Elgar's work was over by 1920 (though he lived until 1934); he wrote all his big music before the end of the First World War. But here at last was a giant in English music. He was soon to be followed by others.

Just before this century began, while Elgar was painfully making his way (he was a self-taught composer), two young men were studying composition with Stanford at the Royal College of Music. They used to meet regularly in a teashop in South Kensington and discuss each other's latest attempts at composition. Their names were Gustav Holst and Ralph Vaughan Williams.

Holst and Vaughan Williams soon became thought of as 'musical twins.' This was largely because, at first, their music did have a kind of 'twinship,' as it had a common parent—folk-music. An important sign of music's reawakening in England at this time was the interest that musicians were showing in the folk-songs and dances which still lived only in the memories of village people. A large number of these were now written down, and it was found that we in this country possessed a rich store of melodies which could be used to give our music a typically English flavour. Holst and Vaughan Williams pounced on these tunes, arranged them for choirs, wrote orchestral rhapsodies on them, and used their melodic twists and turns in their own original music. But soon their ways showed signs of parting. When they were in their early thirties Holst was exploring the mystic poems of the East and setting them to remote, mysterious music. Vaughan Williams, on the other hand, had discovered the poetry of the American Walt Whitman, in which the words pour out warmly and enthusiastically, as if Whitman's ideas could not wait for mere speech to express them.

Away O Soul! Hoist instantly the anchor!
Cut the hawsers—haul out—shake out every sail!
Sail forth—steer for the deep waters only.
Reckless O Soul, exploring, I with thee, and thou
  with me,
For we are bound where mariner has not yet dared
  to go,
And we will risk the ship, ourselves and all.
O my brave Soul!
O farther, farther sail!

With both composers folk-music was forgotten about
for the time being. Holst set oriental poetry to beautiful
music which was like faultless marble—beautiful and
cold; Vaughan Williams matched Whitman's poetry with
warm gusts of sound. They were both exploring the
Unknown in their different ways.

When Holst explored the sounds of the orchestra he
remained far above the earth. In his orchestral suite *The
Planets* he described Jupiter, Mercury, Mars, Saturn,
Venus, Uranus, and Neptune, in sounds the like of which
had never been heard on this earth before.

Vaughan Williams' first three symphonies give us
mood-pictures of the sea, London, and the countryside;
then he appears to express strife (the Fourth Symphony),
unearthly peace (the Fifth), and upheaval and desolation
(the Sixth). In the *Sinfonia Antarctica* (which is based on
the last expedition of Scott of the Antarctic) he evokes
heroism in terms of music, and in the Eighth Symphony
he seems to express the sheer joy of living.

Holst's music seems to be reaching out into Space-ship-
land, and it is a wonderful and exciting experience;
Vaughan Williams catches the moods and feelings of
people and makes them more than life-size. It is not easy
to explain the difference between the music of these two
great men, but we can get near it if we think of the music
of theirs that we know. When we sing the song *Linden
Lea*, or the *Songs of Travel*, or the hymns "For all the
saints" and "Come down, O love divine" we are some-

times surprised to find that the music was written by Vaughan Williams; they seem to be so much part of ourselves that we forget that the man who wrote them died as recently as 1958. When, on the other hand, we sing "Turn back, O man" or "I vow to thee, my country" (the tune from *Jupiter*, in *The Planets*) we feel that somehow we are caught up in a powerful 'march of time'—we sing them as if we can't stop, and don't want to. Holst is the dynamo of English music, generating powerful currents in the shape of unforgettable tunes and stamping rhythms; Vaughan Williams is a kind of sun—just as powerful, but mixing power with warmth in which we can bask.

Both Holst and Vaughan Williams often have the same musical effect on us. For instance, if you listen to Holst's *Hymn of Jesus* and Vaughan Williams's *Sancta Civitas* (*Holy City*) you are likely to find your hair beginning to stand on end with the sheer *electrical* power of the music. And yet with Holst's *St Paul's Suite* and Vaughan Williams's *English Folk Songs Suite* you are back on an English village green, singing and dancing to the old tunes.

These two composers have another great bond. They were both very much in touch with ordinary people. Holst, in spite of his unearthly music, was the very man to get all sorts of people singing and playing; he could go into working-men's clubs, schools, army barrackroom, and in a twinkling of an eye every one would be making music. Vaughan Williams, conducting the country festival at Leith Hill in Surrey, had choirs from country villages meeting year after year to sing great music under his guidance. Wherever there was a need for music this long-lived composer was at hand to supply it. It is enough not to be thought of as a *great composer*, but to have given us songs to sing and pieces to play when we wanted them. Both men are "such as found out musical tunes, and recited verses in writing."

Elgar, Holst, and Vaughan Williams—through their work England became once more a "land *with* music."

Their works do not cross the seas very easily—they are still regarded as too English to appeal to foreign audiences—but they are known and admired everywhere by musicians who take music seriously.

Nowadays we have such a variety of composers working among us that we can make many a concert programme without going outside this country for our overtures, concertos, and symphonies. Here is a list of some of them who have been keeping England on the musical map of Europe:

ARTHUR BLISS, Master of the Queen's Musick. His music is strenuous, brilliant, and very colourful. One of the first composers to write serious music for films, his music to the film *Things to Come* can often be heard as a concert piece. He has written operas, ballets, choral works, chamber music, and a huge piano concerto. Listen to his ballet-suite *Checkmate*, his *Pastoral* for chorus and string orchestra, and his *Colour Symphony*.

GERALD FINZI (who died in the autumn of 1956) was a serious composer who was at his finest when he set good poetry to music. His settings of poems by Shakespeare, Thomas Hardy, Thomas Traherne, and Robert Bridges have given us some of the most expressive songs since Schubert.

HERBERT HOWELLS is carrying on the great tradition of fine church music which we have followed in this book. His music draws fire from the beautiful words of the Book of Common Prayer, the Psalms, the New Testament, and the Mass. His oratorio *Hymnus Paradisi*, written as an epitaph on the death of his twelve-year-old son, is a rare and outstanding work of this century.

JOHN IRELAND (who died in the summer of 1962) delighted generations of pianists with his picturesque piano music. He was almost alone in his ability to write for the keyboard in the true Romantic style of the piano composers of last century. *Ragamuffin*, *Chelsea Reach*, *Amberley Wild Brooks*, and many other pieces are constantly played. There are many songs, too; there can surely be no baritone who has not sung his setting of John Masefield's *Sea Fever*.

EDMUND RUBBRA, who has composed seven large symphonies, shows that he, like Howells, looks back to the great age of Tudor English music, drawing upon its richness of texture and its rhythmic freedom. His music flows in lines of melody like a madrigal, and weaves a noble, darkly coloured pattern of sound.

WILLIAM WALTON has not given us much music, but it is all important. He can write 'noble' music like Elgar, he has a wonderful gift of melody, and he has explored rhythm more deeply than most English composers since Holst. He too wrote an oratorio (*Belshazzar's Feast*) which startled every one with its sheer brutality and power.

Now the twentieth century has more than half passed, it would seem that two composers are making their mark on the larger public just as did Holst and Vaughan Williams forty years ago. These are Benjamin Britten (born 1913) and Michael Tippett (born 1905). Like Vaughan Williams and Holst, they are lifelong friends; both studied at the Royal College of Music, and both are practical performers as well as full-time professional composers.

Britten is a masterly conductor of his own works, and is second to none as an accompanist on the piano. He and Peter Pears, the tenor, have achieved a voice-and-piano partnership which must be unique in the history of concert-giving. The composer's songs seem to have been written especially for the particular and distinctive quality of the singer's voice, and that voice would seem to be created especially for the individual music that Britten writes, so that when they play and sing Britten's songs together one feels that each recital is an event within the history of musical performance. Nor is there any need to look farther afield for a great interpretation of older music, such as a cycle of songs by Schubert. Britten and Pears have made of themselves a single musical instrument, so intimately does each understand the other's musical mind.

Tippett was for eleven years Director of Music at Morley College, a famous place of learning in South London which offers instruction in the arts to working men and women. Holst was also Director in previous years. There, working among ordinary people who merely wished to know a little more about music, Tippett proceeded to change the trends of London's musical taste by introducing the public to the music of composers who had hitherto been for most people merely names in history-books. Monteverde, Gabrieli, even our own composer Purcell, were presented to us through Tippett's activities with a new clarity, and in far greater variety than before.

Britten and Tippett both share the same unshakable principles of humanity towards their fellow-men. Both declined to take part in the Second World War (Tippett spent some months in prison on this account), and whenever an act of injustice or oppression would seem to be committed by Governments or by anyone in authority the voices of both composers will be heard among those raised in protest.

As to their music, the young listener will inevitably come across more of the music of Britten than that of Tippett, since Britten, with his firm belief in the powers of expression that children possess, has written a great deal of music for them to sing and play. By this time many of you will have taken part in *Let's Make an Opera,* based on Charles Kingsley's tale *The Water Babies,* or in *Noye's Fludde,* a dramatized musical story of the Deluge and the Ark, with its load of animals and people. Perhaps you have performed the cantata *St Nicholas,* or sung in the boys' choir in the *Spring Symphony.* In the Suffolk seaside town of Aldeburgh where Britten lives, the inhabitants are accustomed to the sight of busloads of children spilling out into the street, and then into the Jubilee Hall, to be rehearsed by the composer in his latest music for them.

Britten has produced very few works which do not include singers. He receives tremendous inspiration from words—not only English words, but French, Italian, and Latin. They cause him to write exciting melodies which singers delight in singing, and massive choruses which will fill the largest building. His first opera, *Peter Grimes*, a dark tale of tragedy among fisher-folk on the Suffolk coast, was the first British opera to find its way into opera-houses all over the world. His *Serenade* for Tenor, Horn, and String Orchestra was also immediately welcome in other countries, and caused musicians in Europe to agree that here was a composer whose brilliance in finding new sounds would soon be resulting in music of real depth and greatness.

For Britten the year 1962 must always be a major landmark, for then was heard, with profound and universal emotion, the first performance of his greatest work to date, the *War Requiem*. It took place in the new Cathedral in Coventry, the Midland city which was the target of one of the most savage air-raids of the Second World War. The new Cathedral had risen in the centre of this ravaged industrial city, a symbol of the triumph of the human spirit. Great artists had adorned it with paintings, sculpture, and tapestry, and Britten was asked to write some music for it. He immediately saw in this invitation an opportunity to express to the world his intense feeling for "the pity of war." This he did by setting to music the eternal, beautiful words of the Requiem Mass, and into these Latin words inserting solo and duet settings of English war poems by Wilfrid Owen, one of the most sensitive of our poets killed in the First World War. This overwhelmingly powerful and moving work can be compared, if you will imagine it, to the interior of Coventry Cathedral itself; the Latin Mass is the majestic and spacious nave and chancel, and the English war poems are the beautiful and impressive adornments. Before the *War Requiem* appeared there were those critics who were unable or unwilling to see beyond the glittering brilliance and inexhaustible invention of Britten's music. Afterwards, however, these fell silent, except to exclaim, not "How clever!" but "How beautiful!"

The music of Michael Tippett has taken longer to reach us. There is less of it than that of Britten, and very little was composed to make use of mixed forces of professionals, amateurs, and children, such as Britten has constantly given us. All his most important works, however—the two symphonies, the two operas *The Midsummer Marriage* and *King Priam*, the concerto for double string orchestra, the string quartets, the song cycle, and the piano concerto, have delighted all those who have discovered his music with their radiance of sound, their gaiety, and their fascinating rhythms. Tippett has always had an intense interest in jazz and Negro folk-music for the refreshing effect they can have on the rather staid rhythms of European music, and nowhere can this be more enjoyed than in his oratorio *A Child of our Time*.

This work was written in 1941, when the whole of the civilized world had for long watched with mounting horror the oppression of the Jewish people by Nazi Germany, and two years after it had been plunged into war. *A Child of our Time* is based on a notable disaster which overtook the Jews in Germany, five years after Hitler's rise to power. The parents of a young Jewish boy in Paris —a Polish Jew—had been deported from Germany and were stranded on the Polish frontier. In his anxiety for his parents' safety, in a moment of desperation the boy procured a gun and shot dead a German diplomat. This act gave rise to one of the fiercest anti-Jewish outbursts of pre-War days. Thousands of Jews were arrested, and their property wrecked and burnt. As horrified as anyone else at these ugly events, Michael Tippett wrote a dramatic and poetic account of them in his own words and set it to music for chorus, orchestra, and four soloists. The theme of *A Child of our Time* is not "the pity of war" but "the pity of oppression," the tragedy of racial hatred and of man's inhumanity to man. To help convey this, he draws upon those most poignant expressions of slavery and persecution the Negro Spirituals, of which more will be said later. We hear soloists, chorus, and orchestra joining in "Steal away to Jesus," "Nobody knows the trouble I see, Lord," "Go down, Moses," "Oh, by an' by I'm gwin to lay down my heavy load," "Deep River." The effect of these, coming as they do at peaks of emotion in the story, can be as moving as any music of this century.

These two composers, Benjamin Britten and Michael Tippett, have thus far not found it necessary to use any of the new musical languages we have examined in order to express their musical thoughts; their melodies and harmonies are founded on the traditional and familiar musical sounds. But like all creative artists stamped with the mark of greatness, they both can give their individual voices to the simplest music. As one writer put it, both can make the common chord of C major sound different!

Apart from these younger composers there are two rather shadowy figures whose music you might meet quite often. Frederick Delius, born in Bradford, lived most of his life in France; we cannot really own him! But his music has had an enormous effect on later composers. He revelled in beautiful sound and used large orchestras and choruses to get as much of it as possible in all its variety. Listen to *On hearing the First Cuckoo in Spring*; you cannot help delighting in the vivid way in which Delius paints his picture in rich, delicate colours.

Arnold Bax, who was once Master of the King's Musick, was another composer who delighted in sound for its own sake. Listen to his tone-poem *Tintagel*, where he conjures up the rough seas breaking on the Cornish coast. Bax wrote many symphonies, choral works, and songs; and his piano pieces are often played. But he was at his best when he was suggesting a misty, grey scene, and his finest work is perhaps the tone-poem called *November Woods*. He seemed to live in a misty, wintry twilight. . . .

At present the face of music is changing again; we dealt with that in the last Signpost chapter. New ways of writing music are being taken up, and it is good to see that our own composers are not lagging behind the rest of the world. We hope that never again will England be called (as it was for over a hundred years) "the land without music."

12

Music for Entertainment

A LL music is for entertainment. That is to say, all music is to be enjoyed; that is its purpose. But we do not all enjoy the same things. When we go to the cinema some of us like cowboy films but not thrillers; some of us would walk ten miles to see a 'musical' but would not stir out of the house to see a mountaineering film; some of us would want to see a show which would make us laugh; others of us want something that will make us think serious thoughts. We are all enjoying ourselves in our different ways.

Now, broadly speaking, there are four kinds of music:

1. Music that makes us *think* and *feel*. This includes the great church music of all time, the Mozart and Beethoven symphonies, the Wagner operas, the Brahms chamber music, and most of the music of the classical period which has come down to us.

2. Music that we *feel* with our emotions (the Tchaikovsky and Dvořák symphonies, Chopin's piano music, the operas of Verdi, for instance).

3. Music that makes us *move*. This includes dance music of all periods, jazz, swing, the latest 'hits.'

4. Music that *accompanies* our actions (the B.B.C.'s *Music while you work*, the Strauss waltzes we eat to in restaurants, the Sousa marches that brighten up Waterloo Station while we wait for a train, the 'Selections from Musical Comedies' that are so nice to have 'going on' while we read or do our homework).

Now, there was a time when all these four kinds of music were combined. For instance, when Haydn's country-house audiences settled down to listen to a symphony by him they were expected to think and feel in the first movement, to feel the emotions of the slow movement, to tap their feet and nod their heads to the rhythm of the minuet of the third movement, and to think their own thoughts, or even talk, during the frolics of the finale. There was no such thing as 'heavy' music or 'light' music in those days.

But now there is a great gulf between the two. It has been made not by musicians, but by those who think they are. Many people who find that they can sit through a Beethoven symphony without going to sleep are heard to say that they cannot bear to listen to the waltzes of Johann Strauss or the marches of Sousa. As for jazz, it makes them sick! You will never find a true musician taking that attitude. He will go for meat and drink to a Beethoven concert, but he will revel with true delight in the irresistible 'lift' of a Strauss waltz or the exhilaration of a Sousa military march. He will also listen with great interest to jazz, when it is well played by experts, and he will find himself as much moved as any other human being when he hears a simple love-song in the modern style.

Let us see when this gulf began to open. It started with opera. While Wagner was about to shake the musical world with his great operas a Frenchman called Jacques Offenbach was charming every one with his operettas— gay, lighthearted, and rather naughty. Among these were *Orpheus in the Underworld* and *La Belle Hélène*. Whatever was done in Paris was done the day afterwards in Vienna, and the day after that in London. In Vienna Johann Strauss used his supreme gift for catchy dance-tunes in *Die Fledermaus* and *The Gipsy Baron*. In England a serious composer, who had composed "Onward, Christian Soldiers" and *The Lost Chord*, and who was much admired by Queen Victoria, suddenly met a rather unsuccessful lawyer who wrote a little poetry, and with him proceeded to turn out a series of comic operettas which are among the loveliest things in music. The famous partnership of Sir Arthur Sullivan and Sir W. S. Gilbert in time produced *The Mikado*, *The Yeomen of the Guard*, *Iolanthe*, *The Pirates of Penzance*, and all the other Gilbert and Sullivan operas for our lasting delight.

The musical world was beginning to divide itself into two camps: those who went in reverence to the operas of Wagner and Verdi, and those who went to have their ribs tickled by the operettas of Offenbach, Johann Strauss, and Gilbert and Sullivan.

Perhaps it was in England that people first began to say that comic opera was 'worse' than serious music. Sir Arthur Sullivan always wanted to write serious music, and he did indeed produce some oratorios that were a great success with the public. This public included Queen Victoria, who said more than once that Sir Arthur was wasting his talents and his life in writing comic music. But Sir Arthur's oratorios (such as *The Golden Legend*) are now completely forgotten, whereas his operettas, to Gilbert's words, are as fresh and well-loved as ever they were.

The next step was musical comedy. This depended completely on funny dialogue, a good deal of love-interest, attractive scenery and costumes, and lots of catchy tunes. The words did not matter much; they need only be something like:

> I want to be happy,
> But I can't be happy
> 'Till I make you happy too.

But often the tunes were excellent, and they are kept alive year after year in 'Selections,' played on the band-stand or in the restaurant. There is something very lasting in the best of the musical comedy music—*The Desert Song* (Sigmund Romberg), *Rose-Marie* (Rudolf Friml), or *The Land of Smiles* (Franz Lehár). It is 'entertainment-music' at its best. These popular 'songs from the shows' gave rise, however, to a particularly low-grade type of music—the commercial dance-tune. When it became clear that there was an enormous demand for sentimental songs little groups of musical businessmen used to get together and concoct them. They were written so that they could either be danced to or sung in a peculiar way at the back of the throat, known as 'crooning.' This crooning is a very weak sound, and 'crooners' have to have microphones to make themselves heard.

These songs do not just deal with boy-and-girl love. The people who concoct them usually take one sentimental 'feeling' and 'run' it for a time until they feel that the public wants something else. It may be Mother ("It's my mother's birthday to-day"), or Children ("Little man, you've had a busy day"), or even Religion ("I believe"). There is no emotion, however noble and precious, which cannot be turned by these people into good, hard cash, provided the music they put to it is sufficiently vulgar and cheap. Dance-tunes are a sort of musical drug, and in these hectic days there is a huge market for them. Those men and women who sing them in public with sufficient noise and vulgarity are far more popular than the greatest opera-singers, and are paid ten times more money; their gramophone records sell by scores of thousands. It is small wonder, therefore, that many young music enthusiasts have difficulty in deciding what value there is in serious music.

Jazz is a very different matter. It has a long and terrible history, beginning with the shipment of slaves from West Africa to America. These unfortunate men and women brought with them their amazing drum-rhythms and their native tunes, and sang and played them to make their daily toil more bearable. Later they sang of their longing for freedom ("Let my people go!"), and for peace, even in death:

> Deep River! My home is over Jordan;
> Deep River, Lord! I want to cross over into camp-ground.

The West African Negroes took up Christianity with enormous enthusiasm. In their exile they listened to the preacher, prayed together in large, excited crowds, and, of course, sang hymns. These hymns were at first the usual "What a friend we have in Jesus," revivalist type, but they were too tame for these passionate, oppressed people. Before long they were *making them up*—words and music. There was much repeating of lines, and many "Hallelujahs"; the tunes were largely made up of repeated phrases, and there was much stamping and hand-clapping.

Now, all this was going on at the time when Bach, Handel, Haydn, and Mozart were writing their very civilized music. Their music was written on paper so that other people could play the sounds that the composers had thought of. The only performers who were free to make up their own parts were (as we remember) the continuo-player, who filled in the middle parts in Bach's time, the opera-singers who were permitted to put extra 'twiddles' in their songs, and the pianists and violinists who were allowed to make up their own 'cadenzas' at special places in concertos. But in Negro music every one became accustomed to making it all up all the time! As time went on, and the Negroes were made free, they learned how to play instruments and made up their music on them. They naturally chose the instruments that sounded most like human voices. The clarinet was chosen for the high voice, the trumpet for the medium voice, and the trombone for the low voice. With these they had a guitar (later a piano) and, of course, the drums. They would meet in a cellar or in the open—and just begin to play. The really good ones were so sensitive that they knew just what each player was going to do next, and the music surged on of its own accord. It was more than knowing or feeling: it was a strong 'sixth sense' that was generated among them.

The sounds the jazz-players made have never been to every one's liking. To ears that are used to hearing respectable European music they sound rough, vulgar, and ugly, like a primitive carving of a pagan idol. But in its own way jazz makes us *feel* just as strongly as European music, though the feelings might not be quite so worthy of us. For instance, we can feel extremely happy when we stand at the top of a hill, in pleasant company, watching a beautiful sunset; but we can feel just the same happiness *for the time being* after an evening of over-eating and over-drinking at a noisy party. What we must remember, however, is that jazz is genuine; it is an honest way of expressing deeply felt emotion through sound, and it is the only instrumental music that is made up on the spur of the moment by fine, sensitive players.

Jazz became so popular that it was not long before the entertainment world saw that there was money to be made out of it. Then, once again, the damage was done. The honest, crude art of jazz was 'tidied up'; the spontaneously made-up tunes were written down, made to harmonize like well-behaved hymn-tunes, and given to large, civilized dance-orchestras to play. It was just as if a wild part of the sea-coast was given a promenade and an artificial bathing-pool, and called a 'seaside resort.' This music was called 'swing.' Most so-called 'music-lovers' who say that they "can't bear jazz" have not heard any; all they have heard is swing, which they quite rightly associate with crooning and dreadful, sentimental words. It is very rare, however, to find a real musician who does not enjoy the original, honest, clever, emotional sound of jazz. Jazz will never be 'respectable.' It was born in the misery, brutality, and degradation of slavery, and it grew up in the hands of great artists who, however, often lived subhuman lives of drink, drugs, and squalor. But in itself it is real and honest.

It is swing and commercial dance-music, not jazz, which has finally fixed the gulf between light music and serious music. Into the gulf has fallen a good deal of charming ballet-music, many of the exhilarating overtures (such as *Poet and Peasant*, *Light Cavalry*, and *William Tell*), the incidental music and light operas of Edward German, and the touching, artistic songs of such accomplished composers as Jerome Kern and George Gershwin. Many people who wish to be thought musicians say to themselves 'Beethoven or nothing,' as they think that liking light music may let them down in the eyes of the musical world.

What is the answer to this? How best can we use music to make our lives richer? There seems no better way of ending this story of music's progress through the years than to try and 'think aright' about music and ourselves.

Music is to be enjoyed—let us remind ourselves of that. But in return, great music asks us to work for it! While a symphony or a concerto is going on the composer is asking us to use our intelligence to follow what he is trying to say, just as we do when we listen to a great man talking to us. This does not mean that we have to *know* a lot about music; we just have to keep our minds alive. It is different when we go to the local music-hall or variety-theatre. There we will see the audience sitting back and (as it were) saying to the comedian or the entertainer, "All right! Come on, make us laugh!" And woe betide him if he fails. But in the concert-hall Beethoven or Brahms are saying *to us*, "Here are our finest thoughts. We have written them down with great labour, because something inside us said we must. You may care to share them with us." And we enjoy what they have to say *because* of the work we have to do to follow them. In the same way we enjoy climbing a steep mountain and getting to the top. Our enjoyment of great music is the finest enjoyment of all—that which comes through *effort*.

Many people, however, will not go to listen to music unless it is something they know already. They will not attempt to listen to anything new or unusual. Any fathers and mothers will tell you that it is almost impossible to tell a three-year-old child a new bedtime story. If they try there is an instant outcry: "Not that! Tell me *The Three Bears!*" So, with a sigh, off we go again: "Once upon a time there were three bears . . ." So many a concert-goer says to himself, "I shan't go to-night; they're playing some music I don't know by some one I've never heard of." When they say that they are musically at the age of a three-year-old child, but they would be most offended if you told them so!

We cannot call ourselves musical unless we are *adventurous*; for music, like all the finest things in life, is an adventure. We must explore it. If we hear a new piece of music which does not at first appeal to us we must ask ourselves, Is it our fault, or the composer's? And to find out the answer we must listen to it again and again. In that way we are using our intelligence and our judgment in the same way as we do when we are learning how to play cricket, or when we cross a busy street.

There comes a time when we can call ourselves musicians. It is not when we feel we have finally understood this book, or any other book on music. It is when we at last find ourselves thinking, when we see a programme of music we do not know, I don't know this music, and I have never heard of the composer. So I must listen to it and see whether it has anything in it for me to enjoy!

13

Eastern and Tropical Sounds

NEARLY all the music we hear day by day has been written down by the so-called 'white' people of the world: those whose native lands are in Europe, the United States, Russia, Australia, and New Zealand. Just as we all learn our alphabet and our grammar so that we can write what we want to say in our native language, so did the composers of music learn how to write down their music so that it could be played and sung by performers who had also learnt how to read the musical language. The only difference is, of course, that the language of music is international; its notation, its alphabet and grammar, are equally understandable to our fellow-humans in France, Norway, Spain, Hungary, Russia—and to a large number of them in India, China, Japan, and the continent of Africa.

We all know, however, that the countries of Asia and Africa do not by any means depend on 'white' music for their enjoyment. They all have their own means of musical expression, and some of it may mean as little to our ears as a Beethoven symphony may mean to theirs. Yet in these days of exciting exploration of 'non-white' music on the radio, and in films which are based on non-European stories and scenes, it can do us no harm at all to try to understand how this music is put together and performed.

If you went into a music shop in Delhi, Peking, or Tokyo and asked for a volume of Beethoven's piano sonatas you would of course be able to buy it. If, however, you were to say "I want to buy some of that beautiful music at the Indian (or Chinese, or Japanese) wedding I attended yesterday" you would *not* be able to obtain it.

The reason is that the music of these countries is not composed, written down, and published for us to buy, as are the Beethoven sonatas. It is made up, or improvised, by the musicians. But these musicians, singers and instrumentalists, are guided by some basic rules within which they must make their music. Indian musicians, for instance, select two of the main requisites for music-making: a series of notes of varying pitch, like our scales, which is called a *raga*, and a particular series of long and short sounds making a rhythmic pattern (called a *tala*), and within these frameworks they sing and play their songs with infinite variations. There is no attempt to 'harmonize.' The idea of harmony (our third musical requisite) is unknown in Eastern music in our sense, with its several parts or voices playing and singing different tunes but all combining with each other. The excellence of an Eastern musician depends on his ability to think of the most attractive and expressive tunes within the scales and rhythms he has chosen. Nor does the actual *sound* a singer makes give him any special importance. In the East 'a great singer' does not necessarily mean 'a fine voice,' but a great ability to make the very best of his *raga* and *tala*.

The Eastern instruments are far too numerous and varied to be described here, but many of them share a common difference from the instruments we are used to in the Western world. This is in their creation of a more sensitive scale than is possible on our Western instruments. We know from the early part of this book that all the intervals between one note and another in our music are either full tones or half-tones. If you play the scale of C major on the piano you will find that, starting on C, there is a black key between C and D, which will give you a half-tone. And so there is between D and E. But between E and F (and later on, B and C) there is no black key, which means that there is only a half-tone rise in pitch between E and F. Now, try to imagine a tiny black key between those two white ones. If you were to strike that key you would produce a sound higher than E but lower than F. It would be a *quarter-tone*. If you play a stringed instrument you can of course easily produce quarter-tones by moving your finger just a shade away from the note you intended to play. These quarter-tones do not exist in Western music, except in some experiments by Ernest Bloch and some other twentieth-century composers. They cannot be played (obviously) on a keyboard, and there is not yet any official way to write them down on paper. Quarter-tones, however, are used frequently and with most attractive effect in Eastern music. To ears unused to them they produce a plaintive, wailing, 'Oriental' sound which we automatically associate with snake-charming and Hindu ceremonies in the temple.

As we said in Chapter 2, there are three main ways by which we produce music from an instrument: we either strike it (a drum), stroke it (a violin), or blow it (a clarinet). In modern times there are also the two keyboard instruments: the piano, which is 'struck' mechanically, and the organ, which is 'blown' mechanically. Eastern countries all possess stroked, blown, and struck instruments of great variety, though they do not have keyboard instruments. Perhaps the oldest and most universal musical instrument in all civilizations is a struck one—the drum.

The urge to hit something to express joy, grief, excitement, or anger has been with us since the beginning of time. From the tribal drums of the earliest days to the muffled ceremonial drums of State funerals or the highly skilled timpani players of the great orchestras, this exciting sound has been used to provide the final touch of emotion to music. Drums play an immensely important part in non-European music. They exist in so many different forms, and are played in so many different ways, that it would be futile to treat them here in any detail. Let us, then, betake ourselves to a part of the world where the peoples and their cultures have gathered from all parts of the East, who live, work, and make music together, and where we might expect to find the most varied instruments. Let us go to the West Indies—to Trinidad in particular—where Indians, Africans, Chinese, creoles, and British live in harmony, and where was born, only twenty years ago, the most interesting and impressive new musical sound of the century, that of the Steel Band.

The Steel Band combines the playing of ancient Eastern drums with a very modern 'drum' indeed—the oil-drum. All the tunes and harmonies are played on these oil-drums, which are tuned to produce all the notes in the scale. This is done by hammering the top of the drum into a concave shape like a large saucer, and then dividing it up with hammer and chisel into segments, just as one cuts up a round cake. By heating these segments with a blowlamp and pouring oil over them they can be tempered and tuned to produce a particular note. The lowest notes come from the forty-gallon drums, and these are an octave lower than the lowest notes a symphony orchestra can provide. These are known as 'boom-pans.' (The oil-drums are affectionately known as 'pans.') Next to them, giving a higher sound, are the 'cello pans,' which have more notes on them than the boom pans, and are usually grouped in pairs. Next come the 'guitar pans,' higher again, and with still more notes, and finally the treble pans, called the 'Ping-Pongs.' These usually play the tune, and are the same oil-drums, cut down to the size of about six inches in depth, so that they look like large tambourines. All these drums of varying depth are gaily coloured, and are played with varying kinds of drumsticks. The Ping-Pong player, in order to play a tune such as the violins would play, uses two drumsticks which he wields so rapidly that it is hardly possible to hear each individual impact on the surface of the pan. In even a moderately resonant hall, they merge into one continuous note. So too do the impacts of the larger drums; in slow music the whole band can sound like a vast organ.

But the pans, with their ability to play tunes and harmonize with each other, have always had a purely rhythmic group of instruments playing with them—a drum section. This contains drums from all over the East; drums which have their own traditional sounds, Indian, Chinese, African, Japanese. There are drums from China, filled with grain so that they rattle when struck; Japanese drums in the form of an hour-glass, called *tsuzumi*; barrel-shaped drums from India; shallow bass drums from Arabia and the Holy Land. All these have found their way to the Caribbean, and have given their distinctive beats to Steel Band music. Underneath the flowing, sensuous melodies of Caribbean folk-music can be heard the complex pulsating of drums from far and wide; it must surely be the most cosmopolitan orchestral sound in the world.

In recent years the Steel Bands have extended their music from folk-songs and dances to the Western classics. A programme of 'pan music' can now include waltzes by Strauss, Chopin nocturnes, Bach preludes, and—yes!—sonatas by Beethoven and Mozart. This is truly remarkable, since the pan-player cannot read a note of music. Each Steel Band appoints a leader, whose musical ear is so acute and accurate that he can memorize the music from a gramophone record and teach it, part by part, to his men. His skill is phenomenal, and so is his patience. He is so sought after that when a band discovers a leader they often provide him with a house and a job, in order to make sure of his services. Having been taught their parts separately, they meet to rehearse together in the open air, and there, on some waste ground, illuminated perhaps by a single electric bulb hanging from a tree and some kerosene lamps, they set to work. Concentration is fierce, and hardly a word is spoken. From time to time the leader corrects something —"C sharp there, man!" "Too loud, man. Listen to Ping-Pongs!" And so, unsmiling and with complete devotion, they build up a performance of Beethoven or

Chopin accurate to the last semiquaver and played with an astonishing sense of style and mood. Then, resplendent in their uniforms, they fulfil their engagements at the Governor's Residence, the garden parties, and the concert halls.

The early Steel Bands had a rough and turbulent history. The Caribbean, like many other regions, suffered the disorder and hooliganism which immediately followed the end of the Second World War, and the intense rivalry between the bands gave rise to bitter street-fighting and rioting. It has taken many years to obliterate the memory of those early days, and it is only recently that the Steel Bands have established themselves as serious musicians, respectable and dedicated. To see them now, however, immaculately dressed, standing with motionless dignity behind their pans and drums, and to hear this noble, rich, and exciting new sound, is to leave one in no doubt that here is the most important and all-embracing musical event in non-European music for a very long time.

As in the ancient Hebrew days, Eastern music has its roots in two main elements of humanity, religion and the dance. Indeed, both these elements have been inseparable from each other since earliest times, and it must be true to say that all religions except Christianity (which prefers ritual and procession now) have retained the dance as part of their ceremonies to this day. There is a great deal of dancing in the Hindu religion, with ceremonial temple dances, and dances to drive out evil spirits, to send the soul on its journey, and to influence the weather. The sacred dramas in Japan include much dance-movement, and the Moslems propitiated Allah in wild dances performed by their 'dervishes,' austere friars wholly dedicated to religious service. The spread of Christianity among the Eastern peoples has had a 'Westernizing' effect upon their music, and so has the increasing popularity of modern films and of popular dance music. The singing of Protestant hymns and modern dance music has caused many Eastern musicians to make up tunes based very obviously on Western harmonies and scales, so that some of the haunting tunes in Indian or Chinese films can easily be reproduced on the piano with the ordinary chords we are used to in *Hymns Ancient and Modern*. On the other hand, there has often been an 'Easternizing' of European music, due to the movement of non-Europeans throughout the world by emigration or the bondage of slavery. Among the slaves transported from Africa to Trinidad were a great number who worshipped Shango, Lord of Thunder and Lightning. These came from the Belgian Congo, which was converted to Christianity in early days, and stayed so for two hundred years. Then the Congolese went back to Shango—but they took with them the Christian hymns, carols, and chants which they knew. Thus in Trinidad you can hear Shango-worshippers singing hymns to their god using Christian tunes, accompanied by their native drums and instruments. This sounds very strange at first, even disrespectful, until one remembers that it is the music which has been the binding force, the common denominator, of their instinctive desire to worship. Then the tune of "O come, all ye faithful" sung to some primitive verses in praise of the god of thunder and accompanied by wild, off-beat drum rhythms does not offend It quite simply convinces us that if "the twain shall meet"—East and West—it might well be through the benefits of religion and music.

Index